Medical Records
for Lawyers

Medical Records for Lawyers

Ali Malsher
RGN BA MA Solicitor

EMIS Professional Publishing

Publisher's Technical Editor:
Dr Richard Griffin MRCP, Consultant Physician

© Ali Malsher 2002

Published by
EMIS Professional Publishing Ltd
31–33 Stonehills House
Howardsgate
Welwyn Garden City
Hertfordshire
AL8 6PU

ISBN 1 85811 259 1

Typeset by Jane Conway

Printed in Great Britain by Antony Rowe

Dedication

To Leslie

Contents

Preface

This book aims to give a simple introduction to medical records and to provide some general information which hopefully will point the practitioner in a helpful direction when reviewing medical issues. Of necessity, there are areas of medical practice which have been omitted but those that are included are the more common ones which lawyers will have to consider.

Each chapter aims to give a general view including some basic anatomy and physiology but it recommended that practitioners obtain a good anatomy and physiology book or a CD. Some of the books designed for nurses are much easier to understand if starting from little medical knowledge.

The book aims to highlight terms and areas which the practitioner may need to investigate further. It is not an exhaustive list of what tests and treatment should be undertaken but a general overview of the types of symptoms, investigations and care for particular issues – such as infection. It is not a definitive guide but hopefully suggests further issues to consider which may not be readily apparent on first view of the records.

I hope this book succeeds in some of its aims at least. I am conscious that there is a huge variety of knowledge and experience in those dealing with medical issues in law and I am certain that I cannot provide the ultimate guide for all. I hope this is helpful at least.

Lastly I would like to thank Leslie Keegan of 9 Gough Square, who encouraged me in this task and without whom I could not have completed the work. I would also like to thank Andrew whose patience as a publisher has been most helpful!

Chapter 1

Introduction

An increasing number of areas of law involve the use of medical records be they central to the issue of negligence, or relevant to a plea of mitigation. For many lawyers they are a necessary and often incomprehensible evil which should not be left to the medical expert.

Medical records can be understood by individuals without detailed medical knowledge. They can be translated into something equivalent to English and there is a certain logic to the way that they are designed, put together and written. Once the system is understood the records themselves do not often present a problem.

Sorting records

At the outset records should always be sorted. Each practitioner has their own system but it is helpful (not least if you are relying on an expert at some point) to sort them into something similar to the system in which they would be used in the clinical environment. The most convenient way of doing so is to sort them into piles of correspondence, clinical records, operative records (anaesthetic forms, operations notes, pre- and post-operative check lists, theatre records and consent forms), records and results, nursing notes, charts, physiotherapy and miscellaneous records.

Medical and nursing practitioners work differently to legal practitioners in that the most recent note goes on the top of the bundle. However, if further records have to be added at a later stage, this creates problems with pagination. It is easier for the lawyer to have the earliest notes first since updates are often required. It is also easier if pagination is divided into sections (A for correspondence, B for clinical etc.) to allow for additional records in a specific area without causing too much difficulty.

Checking for completeness of records can be a long process. In some cases it is easy to see the second pages of letters which are missing or clinical notes which are incomplete. However, in the results and reports for example, it may not be immediately apparent, particularly if there are substantial records.

The easiest way of checking whether these records are complete is to review the clinical records. The medical team undertake ward rounds in hospital on a regular basis. For an acutely ill patient this may be once or twice a day. For a chronic patient or someone attending for a routine procedure the ward round/medical visit may only be occasional. Whenever the medical team make a decision about what should be done they usually write an entry in the records.

A typical example would be:

– c/o chest pain, SOBOE,
– ?? MI
– For:
   CXR
   ECG
   Enzymes
   ½ hly obs
   review

translated this means:

– complaining of chest pain and shortness of breath on exertion
– possibly heart attack (myocardial infarction)
– for chest x-ray, electrocardiogram (review of heart rhythm), enzyme tests (blood tests which can show abnormal levels of enzyme in the system indicating a heart attack). The nurses are to check (observe) the blood pressure, pulse and (if necessary) temperature every half an hour and the medical staff will review the position.

Therefore the patient would be having blood tests, x-rays and an ECG. There should be a biochemistry form for the blood tests (with results) and/or a message from the laboratories with the results. There should be an x-ray request form which may not be reported on by the radiologist for some days. An ECG might have been performed in the A & E department and there should be a chart detailing the change in pulse or blood pressure.

In some cases the medical team do not get round to writing their requirements down. The nursing staff may have accompanied them on the ward round (and should write down what is due to happen) and individual doctors may discuss with nursing staff further tests which need to be arranged. The nursing records should detail these. This will either be in a message section or in the body of the records as a day entry.

A typical example:

**S/B SHO. Pyrexial. For MSU and sputum.
For Paracetamol PRN**

This would mean that the patient was reviewed by the junior doctor of the team because his or her temperature had risen. Suspecting infection the doctor had requested that urine and sputum specimens be collected. The nursing notes should indicate when this was done and the reports and results section should include a report from the microbiology laboratory detailing the results.

Since the temperature was rising the nursing staff should also have maintained a regular check on temperature and this should be in the charts section. The doctor has also prescribed paracetamol to assist with reduction of temperature of the patient. If it had been given it would be recorded in the drug chart and may also be included in the daily kardex or nursing notes.

The records of other practitioners
Other practitioners have different ways of preparing and completing records. Physiotherapists for example, tend to have their own separate records which show the progress or otherwise of the particular injury or condition. Other therapists – Occupational health, speech and complementary therapists may choose to write in the clinical records. Whenever a referral is made to an alternative teams or practitioners there should be some record either within the body of the clinical records or attached to the records at some point.

Midwifery records
Midwifery (obstetric) records are often included within the body of clinical records rather than forming separate nursing records. There may also be nursing records relating to gynaecology or other matters.

Obstetric records in general are often disorganised. Included in appendix X are examples of the usual types of records which are found and the most helpful order to sort them into. Obstetric records are more involved because they detail the entire gynaecologial and obstetric history but can be understood quite easily once translated. The tests undertaken can be difficult to understand however. Usually there will be a CTG trace (cardiotocograph) which is a graphical depiction of the heart of the baby often compared with the contractions of the mother. These are specialist tests and it is recommended that a simple book analysing CTGs is used to review them.

There are a number of simple books available with good quality diagrams to show the differences in the trace and the possible causes. Likewise while there are a number of typical and common examples of ECGs electrocardiograms (heart monitors) if a detailed analysis is required there are a number of good straight forward ECG books.

Books which are of assistance

It is impossible and expensive to buy books on all areas of medicine and surgery but some basic books are very helpful:

- Anatomy and physiology
- Medical dictionary – nurse's ones are the easiest to understand
- Book on drugs
- ECG and CTG books

Even where information on a specialist area is not available the conditions and problems are often similar albeit a different medical team are dealing with the situation. An infection for example will lead to a rise in temperature, increase in pulse and it should be possible to identify the organism concerned by means of swabs, blood tests and so forth, regardless of the area of body affected.

Likewise whilst there may be different factors which need to be taken into account when an individual is preparing for cardiac surgery rather then orthopaedic, although the essential preparation will be the same. The surgeon still needs to explain the operation, the anaesthetist and surgeon need to be content that the individual can cope with the surgery and the nursing staff will need to complete the usual pre operative checks.

Similarly the post operative complications may not always be the same but often are, regardless of whether the surgery was on the foot or the brain. Much of what appears unknown because it is an unfamiliar area merely requires a review of the underlying condition and some lateral thinking.

Another option is to purchase a CD such as Mentor (see page 339).

Medical terminology and abbreviations

Finally medical terminology is both abbreviated and at first sight incomprehensible. It is possible to translate the terminology so that it can make some sense. Appendix 3 shows the breakdown of particular words. Once the word has been broken into segments it is often simple to work out its meaning.

For example: Hysterectomy – womb/uterus (hyster) and removal (ectomy)

Where abbreviations are found – examine the context and review Appendix 1 which hopefully be able to assist.

The following chapters hopefully provide a review of the usual issues which arise and how they can be interpreted. Medical and nursing practice change constantly but the major conditions with which they deal tend to remain reasonably constant. Included are the more common problems, investigations that are usually undertaken and the treatment or issues which may be relevant on review.

Medical Records

Medical Records

Medical records: Types and meanings

Identification sheets

Identify times and dates of admission – administrative function

Correspondence

See below

Which should include:

- Referral letters
- Correspondence
- Discharge summaries

Ambulance records

Useful for time and date of collection, presentation and time of disposal at hospital.

Clinical records

See below

- Accident and emergency records
- Inpatient/admission records
- Outpatient/clinic records

Operative records

See below

- Consent forms
- Anaesthetic records
- Operation notes

- Day surgery records
- Recovery records
- Pre operative checklists
- Postoperative checklist

Results and reports

See below

- ECG and EMG Scans
- Radiology
- Haematology/Serology
- Biochemistry
- Microbiology
- Virology
- Histopathology
- Cytology
- Ophthalmic and audiology tests
- Respiratory function tests

Nursing kardex

See below

- Admission sheet
- Careplan
- Assessment and evaluation sheets
- Kardex
- Communication
- Discharge summary

Charts

See below

- Observation charts
- Prescriptions and IVI charts
- Fluid balance
- Blood sugar chart
- Peak flow charts
- Urinalysis
- Stool charts

- Fit charts
- Weight charts
- Food charts

Physiotherapy records

See below

Administration and miscellaneous

See below

Correspondence

This should be in date order (medical staff work from back to front so the more recent correspondence would be on the top).

Should include referral letters and discharge summaries, which may be helpful, and self-explanatory. Referral letters are often hand written by GPs and can be difficult to read.

Some medics will note provide correspondence separately but will include them within the bulk of their clinical records. A chronology of events may then be needed to provide an accurate record of dates and treatments.

Correspondence is rarely completed within a few days of admission or discharge. It can often take several weeks for a letter to be dictated and signed. The hand written discharge summaries are quicker but often more difficult to read.

Clinical records

These are the records of the medical staff predominantly although they may include the comments of other professionals including midwives, speech therapist and occupational therapists

They form a pattern of review and record treatment as matters progress.

Clinical records come in various forms:

1. Accident and emergency records
2. clerking

3. inpatient
4. outpatient

To a large extent the records are not dissimilar in that once you can read a set of clerking records you can work round the rest of the clinical records. Inpatient and outpatient records are simply brief reviews of the patient's condition and prognosis and usually include only the facts which have changed or are particularly relevant.

Accident and emergency records

These will usually appear in three main sections – an administrative (usually typed) form which the receptionist often fills on admission to the unit. This includes GP details, next of kin and other pertinent details. It will also record the time of first booking into the department.

The nursing notes usually include those of the triage nurse (a nurse whose role is to review all new patients into the department and decide on priorities). Some hospitals will use codes (red, blue etc or numbers to identify patients requiring different levels of review or treatment). For example a red code may mean the patient needs urgent treatment while a yellow could mean that it is a minor injury and can wait for treatment.

Nursing notes may also include reviews of pulse, blood pressure and temperature and often other tests are completed before medical staff review the patient (for example an ECG for a patient presenting with chest pain).

The clinical records will be in the form of a clerking note (see below) and may include referrals to other medical teams. If this is the case the team who attend to review at the request of the accident and emergency team should also complete a further clerking type review.

Accident and emergency records tend to include all information from the department rather than being separated into sections. Thus the reader should be able to find details of all prescriptions, blood pressure readings, tests and their results in the same two or three pages. They should also include times of treatment which can be more accurate than on general wards where the records may be completed towards the end of a shift.

Often accident and emergency records are kept separate from the general notes and within the department itself. They may also have separate numbering systems.

Clerking notes

These are the initial notes, which detail the patient's history, complaints, and results of examination, diagnosis and treatment. They are often undertaken by a junior doctor and may then be redone (although rarely in the same depth) by a more senior doctor such as a registrar.

They will be followed by the results of tests as they arrive, changes in treatment plans, discussions between medical staff and changes in diagnosis.

Typical clerking follows this pattern:

- Current problem complaining of
- History of current complaint
- Past medical history
- Social history
- Family history
- On examination
- Tests required
- Possible diagnosis
- Treatment and medication plans

E.g.: Freda is admitted with an exacerbation of chronic obstructive airways disease (chronic asthma).

	NAME	Freda Williams
	WARD	3
	HOSPITAL NUMBER:	HS4980

2.2.99	GP referral	
	C/O - SOB over 3/7	
	Productive cough - green sputum	
	PMHx COAD 15 years	
	On nebulisers QDS. Steroids TDS	
	MI 1989	
	Nil else of note	
	SHx Lives alone. NOK in Leeds	
	FHx M & F RIP. 1 child - ♂ 25 yrs	
	O/E - SOB	
	Centrally Cyanosed	
	Clubbing	
	Wheeze and crackles	
	NAD	
	For: ABG	
	CXR	
	FBC	
	Peak flows	
	Sputum for MC & S	
	Admit O/N	
	Δ exacerbation COAD	
	Rx Salbutamol nebs 4 hourly 2 L O2	
	Prenisolone - 40 mgs	
	Bed rest	
	Review on WR	SHO Dr Blue's team 546

Translation

GP referral	As indicated
C/o – SOB 3/7	Complaining of increasing shortness of breath over 3 days
Productive cough	As indicated
PMHx COAD 15 yrs	Past medical history Chronic obstructive airways disease 15 years
Nebulisers QDS	Receiving medication via nebuliser 4 times day
Steroids TDS	Taking steroids three times a day
MI 1989	Heart attack in 1989
Nil else	Nothing else worth noting
SHx	Social history
NOK	Lives alone, next of kin in Leeds
FHx	Family history
M+F RIP	Mother and father dead
♂	Male (1 child male 25 yrs)
O/E SOB	On examination short of breath
Centrally cyanosed	Blue appearance to lips – due to lack of oxygen
Clubbing	Finger tips and nails curl due to same problem
Wheeze and crackles	Sounds of unhealthy lungs

NAD	Nothing abnormal detected
For ABG	To have arterial blood gases analysis (checks oxygen levels in blood)
CXR	Chest x-ray
FBC	Full blood count
Peak flows	Means of measuring respiratory effort
Sputum for MC & S	Microbiology, culture and sensitivity – checking whether infection
Admit o/n	Admit overnight
Δ Exacerbation of COAD	Diagnosis exacerbation of chronic obstructive airways disease
Rx Salbutamol nebs 4hly	Treatment with four hourly nebulisers
2L O_2	Two litres of oxygen
Prednisolone	Steroid treatment increased to 40 mgs per day
Bed rest	As indicated
Review on WR	Review on ward round
SHO	Senior house officer
Dr Blue/546	Consultant name and bleep number for doctor concerned

Further clinical records will usually develop the treatment options and detail and further tests required or results received.

Other terms likely to appear:

WR	Ward Round
S/B	Seen by
D/W	Discussed with
OPA	Outpatient appointment
TTO	Discharge medication
Home	Discharge

Operative records

Include the following:

a. Consent forms

All consent forms should be checked pre-surgery.

They should be signed and dated both by medical staff explaining the operation, and the patient or his/her parent/guardian.

b. Anaesthetic records

Front section

This is similar to a check list. It is for the anaesthetist to review the main areas which will be:

Allergies

Cardivascular system
- problems,
- pulse,
- blood pressure
- and if necessary respirations
- Past medical history

- Medications
- Review of haematology and biochemistry reports

Also on Anaesthetic Charts would be
- previous anaesthetics/operations and any problems
- Family history – i.e. any problems with reactions to anaesthetics which may run in families

Developments in Anaesthetic Records
A patient may be graded I–V on the ASA scale. This is a simple classification adopted from the US. Higher levels *should* receive care from a more senior anaesthetist.

Grade	Definition
I	A normal healthy person
II	Has a mild disease not limiting activity
III	Has a severe disease which limits activity but not incapacitating
IV	Has an incapacitating systemic disease which is constantly life threatening
V	Moribund – i.e. not expected to survive more than 24 hours with or without surgery

Respiratory system
- Problems
- Past medical history
- Medications
- Blood gas levels (if necessary) – demonstrate levels of oxygen and carbon dioxide in the blood

Teeth – loose caps or false teeth

Kidney/Renal system
- Problems
- Past medical history
- Review of biochemistry reports and results
- Medications

Liver/Hepatic system
- Problems
- Past medical history
- Review of biochemistry reports and results
- Medications

Weight and height of patient (calculation of anaesthetic dose)

Pre medication scripted

Back Section

The rest of the anaesthetic record is similar to the observations charts. It will contain details of pulse, blood pressure and respirations alongside anaesthetic, routes of administration and fluids used.

c. Operation note

Generally this is a simple clinical record with detailed account of operation and procedure used. See Surgery section

d. Recovery room records

These show progress post operatively. They are similar in form to general observation charts.

See Surgery section

e. Pre operative check list

This is used to ensure all matters are considered prior to the patient being transferred to the operating theatre.

PRE OPERATIVE CHECK LIST:	NAME WARD PATIENT NUMBER:
1. Name Band	☐
2. Consent form	☐
3. Jewellery	☐
4. Pre operative medication	☐
5. Anaesthetist review	☐
6. X-ray	☐
7. ECG	☐
8. Medical records	☐

f. Post operative check list

**POST OPERATIVE
CHECK LIST:**

NAME

WARD

PATIENT NUMBER:

1. Airways ☐

2. Breathing ☐

3. Observations ☐

4. Respirations ☐

5. Wound check ☐

6. Conscious ☐

7. Records ☐

8. Ward contacted ☐

Results and reports

There are a whole collection of tests and investigations which can be completed to assist with diagnosis and treatment plans.

Mainly they fall into the following categories:

- Radiology and scans
- EMG, EEG and ECG tests
- Haematology – blood tests for checking level of haemoglobin, type of blood and times for blood to clot. Tests to determine the amount of each different type of blood cell. e.g. blood tests to determine the level of haemoglobin, amount of red and white cells, the types of white cells, blood clotting times etc.
- Biochemistry – measurement of the electrolytes and other substances which are also present in blood.
- Microbiology – tests to find which organism may be present (useful for decisions about antibiotic treatment)
- Virology – tests to determine whether a virus is present.
- Cytology – tests for analysis of smear samples from the cervix used for looking for abnormal cells in any sample of body fluid or smear (cervical smear is just one example)
- Histopathology – analysis of tissue which has been removed from the body
- Miscellaneous tests – testing the condition of the lungs, hearing, sight and so forth.

For a detailed review check – **see** Tests and Investigation chapter. Unless there are very few tests it is helpful to separate them and place them in chronological order. It is necessary to check that where a test has been arranged by medical staff in the clinical records, there is a result available.

NB: in G P records tests are often mixed in date order with the correspondence.

Nursing kardex

Nursing records are known as the kardex and are a collection of different records including an admission sheet which should note the pertinent administrative details, past medical history, history of current admission and allergies.

The kardex should also include a section on the activities of daily living (these are a variety of issues which nurses should consider when evaluating the patient on admission and subsequently.) For example some of the more common activities are:

- Eating and drinking
- Breathing
- Elimination (removal of waste products)
- Hygiene
- Mobility
- Sleeping
- Expressing sexuality
- Religion
- Temperature control
- Social activities
- Communication

By using these issues the nurse can evaluate if there is a problem and how it can be dealt with. The care plan should identify the problem, the aim of care and the treatment or care prescribed.

For example a patient who has difficulty with sleeping may be prescribed sleeping tablets in hospital to assist with rest. On a daily basis the kardex is completed to ensure the next shift are aware of the problems and what has happened.

a Nursing kardex

Plain Admission sheet: typical example

Name: Address:	Date: Time:	Past medical history
Next of Kin	Reasons for admission: *NB: Patient's reasons for admission*	Allergies
Date of Birth	Medications	Patient property/disclaimer
Occupation:	Religion:	Primary Nurse
Consultant	GP	Signed

Provides baseline for review of patient during admission

Breathing:	Elimination:	Religion
Eating:	Mobility	Temperature
Drinking	Social/communication	Sleeping

Name: fred egin	Date 2 2 02	Past medical history
Address: 3 Row Street Surrey 0208 545 5454	Time: 11:05	CVA 1989 (stroke) MI 1990 (heart attack)
Next of Kin Mrs Egin	Reasons for admission: Chest pain	Allergies nil
Date of Birth 2 2 23	Medications nil	Patient property/disclaimer signed
Occupation retired post worker	Religion: RC	Primary Nurse Sue Long
Consultant Mr Cardiac	GP Mr GP	Signed Elizabeth nurse

Breathing:	Elimination:	Religion
Needs O2	No problem	practicising
Eating:	Mobility	Temperature
vegetarian	Needs help	fine
Drinking	Social/communication	Sleeping
fine	Deaf L ear (Deaf left ear)	Sleeping tablets on occasions

b Careplans

Many of the careplans are now pre-printed according to the problem of the patient. The final column is for the update reports from nursing staff when events or circumstances change. They are updated, signed and dated by nursing staff.

This is a typical example of a care plan used where the patient has been admitted with a pain control problem:–

Fred is anxious about hospital admission	To reassure and allow him to express concerns	a. allow time to discuss concerns with Fred b. encourage him to express worries c. explain procedures	*Fred aware of tests and has discussed with medical staff. No longer anxious S/n Brown 2.2.02*
Fred is suffering pain	To be pain free	a. encourage Fred to report pain b. look for non verbal signs c. administer analgesia as charted d. report break through pain to medical team	*Codeine scripted qds 2.2.02 S/N Brown* **Reduced to co proximal 3.2.02 S/N White**
Fred is having difficulty with sleep	To sleep effectively	a. encourage Fred to report problems b. to discuss concerns with Fred to ease worries c. medication as scripted d. keep routine at night as near to Fred's normal routine if possible	*Nitrazepam scripted with good effect 2.2.02 S/N Brown* **No longer needed. Sleeps well 3.2.02 S/N White**

The Kardex proper

This is the daily record kept on each shift covering the events. Where care has been as per the plan nurses often record "care as plan" and nothing else.

Date		Signed
2.2.02	Admitted with poor pain control. Dr Medic's team. Diagnosis.	S/N Abbey
am	For best rest Fluids and pain relief. NOK informed	
2.2.02	Eating well. Seen by Dr Junior Medic. Scripted for Codeine	S/N Church
p.m.	Wife visited	
Nocte	Complaining of pain in left leg. Dr Very Junior Medic informed.	
	Unable to sleep. Complaining of noise from other patients in ward	
	Dr Very Junior Medic attended – scripted for Nitrazepam	S/n
	Given with good effect	Cathedral
3.2.02	Codeine required at 11:00. care as plan	
am	Ward round with Dr Senior Consultant. To reduce Codeine to co-proximal. Codeine scripted PRN	S/N Church

Date		Signed
Pm.	Care as plan. Long discussion re: pain relief. Feeling better. Wife visited for long period seemed tearful but cheered up. Eating and drinking well. No codeine required.	S/N Abbey
Nocte	Slept well. Care as plan	S/N Cathedral
4.3.02	Ward round – for discharge. TTOs scripted. NOK informed	S/N Abbey
a.m		

Key:

TTO   To take away/out – discharge medication
PRN   as needed
NOK   next of kin

c Evaluation or Communication Sheet

Some nursing records also include an evaluation or communication sheet. The evaluation sheet will record how matters are progressing generally. The communication sheet will include discussions with medical staff and other professionals, instructions and details of problems relayed to the doctors +/or family.

Charts

These are the means by which a patient's condition is subject to review by nursing and medical staff. The more common charts used are:

a. observation charts – testing for pulse, temperature, blood pressure and respirations.
b. Prescription charts

c. Fluid balance charts

a The Observation chart

The first review of an observation chart will normally consider the pulse, whether it remains constant, whether it is fast or slow, irregular, thready or there is a difference between the heart rate itself and the pulse present in the wrist.

Pulses

This is the process where the pulsations of an artery can be felt through the skin. Normally these are taken by placing two fingers over the radial pulse in the wrist but in fact pulses can be taken wherever a reasonable sized artery can be felt near to the skin surface.

Range of pulses

The normal range of the pulse is age dependant:

Age	Range
Infant – 0–6	90–160 beats per minute
Child > 6 years	80–120 beats per minute
Adult female	60–100 beats per minute/average 80
Adult male	55–95 beats per minute/average 75

Sites of pulses

Temporal	Head
Carotid	Neck
Brachial	Just above the elbow on the inner aspect of the arm
Radial	Wrist
Ulnar	Wrist
Femoral	Groin
Popliteal	Top section of leg just above knee – inner aspect
Posterior tibial	Back near ankle
Dorsal pedis	Known as pedal pulse – top of foot

It is also possible to take the pulse by listening to the heart itself via a stethoscope (often known as the APEX pulse).

Where problems with the heart are suspected and there is an indication that the heart rate does not effectively translate into a similar pulse in the wrist two pulses are taken simultaneously, these are the radial pulse and the apex pulse (taken by listening to the heart rate by placing a stethoscope over the heart). Two nurses are needed for this procedure.

An increase in the pulse or heart rate can be due to a number of factors including:

a. anxiety
b. infection
c. injury
d. increased temperature
e. medication
f. cardiac conditions

Where there is a sudden or substantial increase in the pulse it is usually taken again and at frequent intervals until matters are resolved or the underlying cause is identified.

Blood pressure

This is the means by which the pressure of blood circulating within the system can be measured. Blood pressure is measured in mms of mercury (Hg).

The two measurements used are:

- **Systolic**
  Pressure at the time of the heart beat where the blood is pushed through the heart and into the main artery to the body.

- **Diastolic**
  Pressure when the heart is at rest between beats.

  120/80 = 120mm Hg (mercury) is when the heart beat has pushed the blood through into the aorta/ 80 mm Hg when the body is at rest.

Blood pressure will be raised by:

a. cold weather
b. some kidney diseases

c. other conditions can lead to this problem including:

a. anxiety and pain
b. some hormonal diseases
c. some complications of pregnancy
d. some abnormalities of the blood vessels
e. usually no cause is found, when it is called "essential hypertension"

Blood pressure is measured by a SPHYGMOMANOMETER (SPHYG for short). The nursing or medical staff listen for two things: the first, similar to a thud, indicates the start of the systolic; the second is a gradual disappearance of sound which indicates the diastolic.

Normal Blood Pressure

Age	Systolic (At peak)	Diastolic (at rest)
new-born	65–90	30–60
Infant 1 year	65–125	40–90
Infant 2 years	75–100	40–90
Child 4 years	80–120	45–85
Child 6 years	85–115	50–70
Adolescent 12 years	95–135	50–70
Adolescent 16 years	100–140	50–70
Adult 18–60	110–140	60–90
Adult 60+	120–140	80–90

These are approximate ranges depending on the health of the individuals concerned. In addition, as individuals become older so the systolic tends to rise. It is not unusual for an otherwise healthy older adult to have a systolic pressure of 150 or 160. However if the diastolic is also raised there should be cause for concern.

Postural problems

In some cases blood pressure will fall when an individual stands up. This is known as postural hypotension. To test for this, blood pressure needs to be taken when lying down followed by standing upright. If postural hypotension is present the blood pressure will drop some 20–30mm/Hg (mm of mercury) and the pulse will increase by 10–25 beats per minute.

False readings
This can be common with inexperienced staff. It is possible that the cuff used to restrict the blood flow through the arm is too loose, too tight, too narrow or too wide.

Respirations

These are usually recorded with children, but in many adult cases they are not recorded routinely. The exceptions are post-surgery or where there is evidence or a possibility of respiratory difficulties.

Normal range of respirations
Baby   − 30–60 respirations per minute
Child   − 20–30 respirations per minute
Adult   − 10–20 respirations per minute.

Assessment of Respirations
Respirations are assessed by reviewing:

- Depth
- Rhythm
- Effort (common for chronic asthmatics and bronchitics to make significant effort
- Expansion – chronic asthmatics etc will use the entire lungs to breathe
- Symetrical or asymmetrical
- Cough – productive (specimen of sputum may be required)
- Auscultation – sounds of the lungs: wheeze, crackles no sounds

Use of oxygen
Oxygen will be prescribed generally in the prescription chart but the following levels apply:

1L oxygen (O2)	24% Oxygen
2L	28%
3L	32%
4L	36%
5L	40%
6L	44%

NB Patients with chronic respiratory problems generally should not receive more than low doses of oxygen. All oxygen should be given with caution.

Temperature control

Normal temperature is:
- Adult 36–37 degrees C
  >37 degrees Pyrexial
  >38 degrees Hyper pyrexial
  <36 degrees Low
  <35 degrees Hypothermia
- Child/neonate – requires assistance to maintain reasonable temperature
  Normal range 36.5–37 degrees

Causes of high temperature:
a. Excessive clothing
b. Excessive outside heat and insufficient control of body heat
c. Infections – most common cause
d. Injury
e. Stress

High temperatures caused by infection, may form patterns which suggest underlying conditions. They may SPIKE at particular times of day (increase significantly).

Low temperatures – particularly in the hypothermia range – are emergencies and require urgent treatment to slowly increase the body temperature

Sites of taking temperature:
- Axilla — under arm, less accurate
- Oral — in mouth more accurate but uncomfortable
- Rectal — Commonly used in babies
- Via finger — Mechanised temperature review used in theatres and in ITUs mostly.
- Tympanic — from the ear canal, accurate and comfortable.

Prescription charts

These will include:

- Patient name
- Ward name
- Consultant name
- Hospital Number
- Date of birth
- Allergies

They will also include the following four sections:

a. Regular medications
b. Stat doses (medications given once – for example pre-medications for surgery)
c. PRN or "as needed" medications such as sleeping tablets and mild painkillers
d. Intravenous fluids and additives

For example:

Section of chart

	TIMES								
DATE start 2/2	6 AM	2/2 GH	3/2 GH	4/2 GH	5/2 GH	6/2 GH	___	___	
PRESCRIPTION Flucloxacillin	10 AM								
DOSE 250 mgs	12 PM	hy	pds	hy	pds	hy			
ROUTE po	2 PM								
TIME qds/5 days	6 PM	pds	hy	pds	hy	pds			
DR: Junior medic	10 PM	GH	GH	GH	GH	GH			

Translated the example above means that:–

- Flucloxacillin
- Prescribed for five days.
- Four times a day
- Dose of 250 Mg
- Junior doctor prescribed.
- Given in tablet form.
- Signed as given by GH on night shift @10 pm and 6 am times
- Signed as given by S/n HY and PDS on morning and afternoon shifts

For details of the drugs and medications see chapter on Medications.

Fluid Balance Charts

These charts are the means by which nursing staff record what fluids enter and output a body over a 24 hour period.

Example chart

Freddie:
Ward 3
Date of Birth: 24.1.63
Date of chart: 2.2.1999

Input   **Output**

Time	Fluid	Amount	Total	Site	Amount	Total
1:00				HNPU		
2:00				HNPU		
3:00				HNPU		
4:00	Tea	Sips	Sips	Vomit	200 mls	200 mls
5:00	Water	Sips	Sips	Drain	200 mls	400 mls
6:00	Tea	120 mls	120	Drain	140 mls	540 mls
7:00	IV N/S (start)	1L (8 hours)		PU	300 mls	840 mls
8:00				Drain	100 mls	940 mls
9:00	H$_2$O	100 mls	220+	Drain	60 mls	1,000 mls
10:00				Drain	20 mls	1,020 mls
11:00	Tea	120 mls	340+			
12:00	Milk	100 mls	440+	PU	550 mls	1,570 mls
13:00						
14:00						
15:00	IV N/S	1L (8 hours)	1,440			
16:00	Tea	120 mls	1,560	PU	200 mls	1,770 mls
17:00						
18:00	Coffee	120 mls	1,680	PU	250 mls	2,020 mls
19:00	Water	100 mls	1,780			
20:00						
21:00	Tea	120 mls	1,900	PU	280 mls	2,300 mls
22:00				Drain	100 mls	2,400 mls
23:00	IV discontinued		2,900			
24:00				PU	200 mls	2,600 mls

Total Input   2,900   Total Output: 2,600 mls
Balance (+ balance of 300 mls)

Key:

N/S   Normal Saline – fluid for infusion for simple re hydration or maintaining hydration in patient
HNPU   Has not passed urine
H$_2$O   Water
PU   Passed Urine

Other charts

Fit charts

These record type and frequency of fits, also whether there are any signs received per fit and actions of the person while having fit.

Stool charts

These record frequency, amount and description.
(**see** Tests and Investigations chapter – Microbiology section)

Urinalysis charts

These are usually done to show levels of sugar in urine but sometimes to show protein or blood or ketones in urine

Peak flow charts

These test the level of respiratory effort in exhalation. They are used for asthmatics and individuals with chronic obstructive airways disease. They measure peak flows before and after medication (usually nebulisers) to check severity and whether there is a difference and how effective the medication can be.

Normal adult range: 400 +.
Chronic asthmatic in severe exacerbations may have range of 100–150.

Vomit chart

This records the amount, frequency and appearance of vomit where an individual has a particular problem. They are not used generally in cases where there are only one or two episodes.

Description	Possible condition	Issues
Undigested food	Oesophageal stricture	Restriction in the gullet
Blood	Upper GI bleeding	Could be serious
Coffee ground appearance	Upper GI bleeding	Could be serious
Bile	Intestinal obstruction	May require surgery
Faecal contents	Lower Intestinal obstruction	May require surgery
Projectile	Pyloric stenosis (restriction near stomach) Also sign of raised pressure in brain	Often urgent attention required – particularly with increased pressure
Early morning	Alcohol Pregnancy	Pregnant women can also vomit at other times

Blood sugar charts

These are used for suspected or diagnosed diabetics where the condition is uncontrolled or the patient is undergoing a procedure which will affect the control of diabetes for a temporary period.

A pin prick of blood is taken from the finger or ear, and placed on a blood sugar monitoring stick (E.g.: diastix) to measure the Blood Sugar level.

The usual adult range is 3–7 mmols. There is a problem if:–

- <3 mmols – hypoglycaemic – requires sugar substance to increase level and prevent coma
- > 15 mmols – too high

When the level gets too high i.e. hyperglycaemic, a coma will also occur.

When the blood sugar is uncontrolled it is extremely dangerous and can result in death. This is more likely to occur with insulin dependent diabetics than those controlled by medication or diet.

Weight charts

Most patients are weighed routinely on admission. Some are weighed daily depending on their condition: for example if there is Cardiac failure, or liver and kidney failure. Pregnant women are frequently weighed.

Neurological charts

See Neurology section

G P records

G P records are often still placed within small envelope type folders known as Lloyd George folders.

These include all the medical records relating to a patient but many GPs now also keep records on computer systems such as those produced by EMIS. A printout can be much easier to read because it often does not include all of the usual handwritten abbreviations.

The following table shows an example of a GP record made on small card. The translation is then shown in the second table. N.B. Entries are often not in chronological order and cards are completed on both sides.

Example

5/6/90	A	C/o D&V. ↑ temp. 5/7	
		O/e- nad - Δ GI - advice re: N B M 1-3/7, ↑ fluids	
14.2.94	V	C/o pain in throat. ↑ 3/7 unable swallow, weak	
		O/e - red and inflamed. Temp 38 degrees	
		Swab, bloods.	
		Advised BR Abx - penicillin qds 250 mg	
		Paracetamol PRN and fanning	
16.3.96		Smear - NAD	
24.3.97	A	C/o back pain LS – tender – HO recent fall – bruising. Advised re: BR and NSAID.	
29.3.97	A	Still suffering - refer A & E - XR	

A – attendance
V – visit at home required

Translation

5.6/90	Attendance at clinic	Complaining of diarrhoea and vomiting with increased temperature for 5 days
		On examination nothing abnormal detected. Diagnosis of gastro-enteritis. Advised to eat nothing for one to three days and increase fluid intake.
14.2.94	Visit to home	Complaining of pain in throat. 3 days unable to swallow. Weakness.
		On examination red and inflamed throat. Temperature very high.
		Throat swab taken and bloods
		To start on antibiotic treatment. Penicillin 4 times a day @ dose of 250 mg
		Paracetamol to bring temperature down as needed. Use of fan
16.3.96		Smear result – nothing abnormal detected
24.3.97	Attendance at clinic	Complaining of back pain in the lumbar sacral position. History of recent bruising. Advised on bed rest and non steroid anti inflammatories
29.3.97	Attendance at clinic	Still in pain – refer to accident and emergency for x-ray

GP records will also include:

1. Examination or clerking sheet providing basic review of history
2. Possibly a chronology of important medical events such as operations
3. An immunisation record for children and possibly some adults

4. A separate sheet detailing prescriptions particularly if patient suffers from chronic condition
5. Correspondence
6. Results and reports

656é8

Chapter 3

Common Medical Tests and Investigations

Common Medical Tests and Investigations

Medical Tests and investigations tend to fall into one of the following categories:

- Blood tests
- Other specimens and samples
- Scans
- Contrast dyes
- Scopes
- Other general tests
- Gynaecology and Obstetric tests
- Physical examinations
- Respiratory tests

Blood tests

Haematology

Blood has a number of constituents. It is made of plasma in which a valume of different cells are suspended. Plasma constuitutes approximately 55% of the blood volume while the cells consitute the remaining 45%

Plasma includes

- Proteins:
  albumin (see biochemistry), fibrinogen, clotting factors,
- Mineral salts
  (Calcium, sodium bicarbonate, phosphorus, potassium, magnesium, sodium chloride and other – see biochemistry)
- Nutrients from food
- Waste materials
- Uric acid, urea and creatinine (see biochemistry)
- Hormones

- Enzymes
- Antibodies
- Gases

Cells

There are three varieties of cell:

White Cells – LEUKOCYTES

Function – put simply the function of the white cells is to protect the body from foreign material. They develop specific protective capabilities and allow for the passing on to the next generation of cells the ability to repeat the process.

They are made up of:

- Granulocytes   – Neutrophils
                      – Eosinphils
                      – Basophils
- Monocytes
- Lymphocytes

Red cells – ERYTHROCYTES

Function – to contain haemoglobin which eventually combines with oxygen and transports this to the various organs and muscles in the body.

Blood groups are associated with red cells.

Platelets – THROMBOCYTES

Function – working by clotting its function is to assist repair of damaged tissue.

There are a large number of clotting factors and conditions.

Cells	Range	Significance or Issues
Haemoglobin	Male – 13-17.7 g.dl-1 Female – 12.2-15.2 g.dl-1	Reduced level results in less oxygen being taken to cells. Number different types of haemoglobin when considering blood disorders: some of these also require special tests to detect them.
Mean cell haemoglobin (MCH)	27–32 pg	Reduced in iron deficiency anaemia (microcytic anaemia) and thalassaemia
Mean cell haemoglobin concentration (MCHC)	32–35g.dl-1	May be diminished in a number of anaemias
White cell count (WCC)	4-11 × 10 9/L	Increased levels – response to infection, tissue damage or attack on immune system.
Basophils granulocytes	<0.01-0.1 × 10 9/L	Significantly increased in some forms of leukaemias and myelofibrosis
Eosinophil granulocytes	0.04 – 0.4 × 10 9/L	Increased in skin disorders and pulmonary disorders associated with hypersensitivity or allergies, some malignant disorders such melanoma and lymphoma
Lymphocytes	1.5 – 4.0 × 10 9/L	Particularly increase in response to viral infection or chronic infection such as TB
Monocytes	0.2 – 0.8 × 10 9/L	Involved in immune responses – increased levels at time when immune system under attack
Neutrophil Granulocytes	3.5 – 7.5 × 10 9/L	Rises in bacterial or viral infection **or** as a result of tissue damage
Plasma volume	40–50 ml/kg-1	
Platelet count	150–400 × 10 9/L	Bleeding uncommon with levels more than 50 × 10 9/L. Reduced platelet production THROMBOCYTOPENIA – easily bruises, nose bleeds (epistaxis) and menorrhagia (heavy periods)
Serum B12	See biochemistry	

Cells	Range	Significance or Issues
Erthyrocyte Sedimentation Rate (ESR)	< 20 mm in 1 hour	Raised rate indicates possible infection or degenerative disease. Can be low in congestive heart failure or sickle cell. Increase naturally with age, pregnancy (after 3 months) and be affected by steroids and the contraceptive pill
Bleeding time	3–10 min	
Partial thromboblastin time (PTT/APTT) (activated PTT)	30–50 seconds	Prolonged in some clotting disorders e.g. some types of haemophilia Used to monitor intravenous heparin therapy in hospitals to ensure correct dosages when treating blood clots
Prothrombin time (PT)	1.0–5.0 seconds	Prolonged in some clotting disorders e.g. vitamin k deficiency, liver disease Used to monitor warfarin therapy when used to reduce blood clotting. It is expressed as the INR (International Normalised Ratio) as a number with 1.0 being normal clotting. Normally patients on warfarin should have an INR greater than 2.0 but less than 5.0

Common Haematology Tests

Hb, FBC (full blood count), WCC (White cell count), ESR, PTT/PTTK/PT.

All ranges are approximate.

Biochemistry

These are tests for elements (often minerals) within the body which may have an effect on the way systems work, or, may suggest the underlying cause of a condition. Many are taken and tested by taking a blood sample. The ranges below are those for an average adult using a blood sample. (However often tests are undertaken by analisying the urine and the levels which are found in urine are different.)

These tests are known usually as U & E s – urea and electrolytes.

Substance	Normal Adult Range		Issues
Albumin	35–55g/l	Serum albumin is sensitive guide to chronic liver disease. Increased level – may be due to dehydration or diabetes insipidus. Low levels – may be due to chronic illness, overhydration, malnutirition and cancer which has spread (metasteses)	Falling blood levels – poor prognostic indicator – liver
Alanine Aminotransferase (ALT)	3–60 IU/l	Increased level – may be due hepatitis, cirrhosis, obstructive jaundice. Low levels – Vitamin B6 deficiency	Specifically used for liver disease
Alkaline Phosphatase	30–120 IU/l	Elevated levels – disease of liver, lung pancreas and bone. Elevation pronounced with liver and gall bladder conditions such as tumours and broken bones. Low levels may be due to problems with parathyroid gland, pernicious anaemia.	Many drugs, conditions and chemicals which affect determination. Care with specimen
Aspartate aminotranserase (AST)	8–40 IU/l	Elevation – myocardial infarction (heart attack), heart failure, central nervous system disease, eclampsia. Low levels may be due to vitamin B6 deficiency and terminal stage of liver disease.	May be used for liver disorders but non specific. With Heart attack – check when peaks!
Bicarbonate (HCO3)	22–30 mmol/l	Acts as a buffer ensuring concentration of hydrogen cells inside and outside of cells remains constant	See acidosis

Substance	Normal Adult Range		Issues
Bilirubin	3–20 micromols/l	Predominantly created by breakdown of red cells in liver. Excreted in urine. High level – jaundice, liver disease	
Calcium	2.12–2.65 mmol/l	Increased level: (signs) deep bone pain nausea constipation. May be due to bone secondaries from cancer, problems with parathyroid gland. Reduced level: (signs) Abdominal cramps, tingling. Muscles spasms, convulsions. May be due to kidney failure, pancreatitis.	Assess magnesium levels. Check parathyroid hormone (PTH) levels, cancer NB lab reports will provide a calcium level and a corrected calcium level. The corrected one must be the one used.
Cholesterol	3.9–6.5 mmol/l (rough guide)	Can develop into gallstones and predispose to heart disease. Increase may be due to diabetes mellitus, pancreatitis, problems with thyroid. Low level may be due to infection, heart failure or malignancies	High levels can be heridary
Creatine kinase	Male 25–195 IU/l Female 25–170 IU/l	a. Relatively specific enzyme for damage to heart muscle after heart attack b. Any muscle damage e.g. a bad fall or crush injury c. Muscular dystrophy-elevated levels of Creatin phosphokinase	a. Peaks at 1–2 days. False positive results from muscle and brain disorders b. differing levels apply to Creatine phosphokinase
Creatinine	60–150 micromols/l	A high level may indicate kidney problems or urinary obstruction	Also indicates urinary obstruction, dehydration

Substance	Normal Adult Range		Issues
Ferritin	Men 15–400 ng/ml Women 10–200 ng/ml	Reduced if short of iron – can be increased by any infection or severe illness	
Gamma-glutamyl transferase (gamma GT)	Male 11–51 IU/I Female 7–33 IU/I	Rises in liver diseases especially related to alcohol	
Glucose (fasting)	4–5.5 mmol/l	Level of sugar in blood – see hyperglyacaemia and hypoglycaemia	Important measurement – particularly if consciousness level reducing
Iron	Men 15–31 micromol/l Female 14–30 micromol/l		
Lactate dehydrogenase (LDH)	120–280 IU/I	Increased level – heart attack, anaemia, leukaemia, kidney or liver disease, brain damage	Check when peaks with heart attack! peaks 48–72 hours
Lead	<1.2 umol/l–1	Increased level – signs – nausea, abdominal pain, diarrhoea and blood in vomit (Haematemesis)	Poisonous effect! – severe cases liver damage and coma
Luteinising Hormone (LH) pre menopausal	6–13 U/I	07–1.1mmol/I–1	
Magnesium		*Increased level:* lethargy, respiratory problems, coma *Low level:* Tremors, cramps, tachycardia, hypertension, confusion	Assess calcium level, parathyroid problems, cancer
Phosphate	0.8–1.45 mmol/l		Important part of most cell systems

Substance	Normal Adult Range		Issues
Potassium	3.5–5.0 mmol/l	Increased levels – can cause cardiac arrythmias and death. Caused by kidney failure, diabetic ketoacidosis and drugs. Low levels – can cause weakness, cardiac arrythmias and death. Caused by drugs, fluid loss e.g. diarrhoea	Needs urgent evaluation and treatment if symptommatic
Sodium	132–145 mmol	Increased levels – sign of dehydration and fluid loss, diabetes insipidus or diabetes mellitus. Reduced levels also seen in dehydration and also a drug side effect and in lung and brain problems as well as after surgery. Low levels can cause confusion, fits, coma and death	Need careful evaluation and correction – correcting the levels too quickly can increase the complications
Thyroxine Stimulating Hormone (TSH)	0.008–6.0 mU/l	Regulates release of T4 and T3 into blood	Signs of over production of thyroid hormones – nervousness, short attention span, increased heart rate and blood pressure, skin warm and moist, weakness and fatigue. Signs of reduced levels – lethargy and headaches, reduced heart rate and blood pressure, lowered respiratory rate, weight gain and skin cool

Substance	Normal Adult Range		Issues
Thyroxine (T4) (Free thyroxine) (Free T4 or fT4)	10–20 nmol/l	Release by thyroid gland. Low level in underactive thyroid. High level in overactive thyroid.	As above NB: numerous other symptoms
Tri-iodothyronine (T3)	1.2–3.0 nmol/l	Hormone – as above	As above
Troponin I	Normal range varies	Released from the heart after a heart attack or bad angina attack. Rises 6–12 hours after the pain. Oftern used as a test to rule out cardiac causes of chest pain.	
Urea	2.5–6.7 mmol/l	End product of protein metabolism (use of proteins by body)	
Uric acid	Male – 210–480 micromol/l Female – 150–390 micromol/l	Increased levels may be due to gout, kidney failure, reduced activity in thyroid gland (hypothyroid). Low levels may be due to large doses of Vitamin C, medications	
Vitamin B12	200–900 ng/ml	Signs of deficiency – neurological problems, pernicious anaemia	Absorption can be measured by the Schilling Test

Liver Function Tests L F T

Will include the usual biochemistry results

Also include:

Serum (Blood) bilirubin levels
Serum (Blood) Aminotransferases – alanine and aspartate
Serum (Blood) alkaline phosphatases
Serum (Blood) gamma glutamyl transpeptidase (Glutamyl transpeptidase)
Prothrombin times

Other Tests

These may include

Urea and electrolytes (U and Es)
which are   urea
             creatinine
             bicarbonate
             sodium
             potassium

and

Cardiac enzymes
which are   creatinine kinase
             AST
             Troponin

Blood Gases

A third type of blood test which is very common is the arterial blood gas (ABG).
This is taken from an artery – usually the pulse at the wrist and measures the level of oxygen, carbon dioxide and acid in the blood.

Substance	Normal Adult Range	
Partial pressure of oxygen (pO_2) (P_aO_2)	12–13.5 kPa	Low level indicates lack of oxygen in the blood because of lung or cardiac problems
Partial pressure of carbon dioxide (pCO_2) ($paCO_2$)	5–6 kPa	Low level in hyperventilation. High level in failure to ventilate the lungs properly. Caused by lung diseases, drugs and excessive oxygen therapy. Causes drowsiness and coma.
pH	7.40	Low pH indicates increased acid levels (acidosis). May be due to increased pCO_2 or any serious illness.

Other specimens

Microbiology

The role of microbiology is to detect the organisms which may be present in particular body fluids and specimens. This allows for the correct diagnosis to be made and the correct treatment (particularly in the case of anti-biotics) to be provided.

Terminology

- EMU   Early morning urine specimen
- HVS   High vaginal swab
      Test for variety of infections
- MSU   Mid stream urine specimen
- Sputum   Sent for cytology – this should be sent for culture

Stool specimens and appearance

Characteristic   Issues and importance

- White or clay colour   Consider bile obstruction
- Black or tar like appearance   Likely to be blood or iron. Upper gastrointestinal tract bleeding.

- Red — Fresh blood – lower gastrointestinal tract, some vegetables – beetroot!
- Green/yellow — Infection
- Pale — Poor absorption of fats
- Disagreeable smell — Infection or contains blood
- Frequency — Infection, could be related to high fibre content in diet
- Less than 1 × three days — Constipation – can also result from dehydration and medication
- Hard — Constipation or lack of fluids, dehydrated
- Loose — Diarrhoea, some medications
- Watery — Infection
- Liquid — Infection or impacted bowel so that only limited amounts of faecal substance can get through

Common Organisms and Infections

Microbiologists will be able to identify the organisms using various techniques including varieties of the same group such as staphylococcus. Different strains of organisms produce different patterns of disease and require individual antibiotic treatment.

Infection	Organism (pathogen)
Septicaemia	Coliforms
	Enterobacter species
	Staphylococcus Aureus
	Streptococcus species
Bacterial meningitis	Streptococcus pneumoniae
*neonates – large number of organisms will cause meningitis	Neisseria meningitis Haemophilus influenzae
Acute endocarditis	Staphylococcus Aureus
	Staphylococcus epidermis
	Streptococcus pyogenes
	Gram negative bacilli
Enteric Fever	Salmonellae

Infection	Organism (pathogen)
Cholecystitis	Coliforms
	Streptococcus faecalis
	Salmonellae
Food poisioning	Salmonellae
	Clostridium welchii
Gastroenteritis	Salmonellae
	E coli
Peritonitis	Coliforms
	Streptococcus faecalis
	Clostridia
Post operative wounds	Staphylococcus aureus
	Pseudomonas aeruginosa
	Coliforms
Urinary tract infections – cystitis	Coliforms
	Proteus
	Streptococcus faecalis
Nephritis	Gram negative bacilli
Respiratory tract	Haemophilus influenzae
	Streptococcus pneumoniae
	Staphylococcus aureus
Tonsillitis	Streptococcus pyrogenes
Otitis media	Streptococcus pneumoniae
	Streptococcus pyrogenes

N.B. Resistant bacteria "superbugs" are beyond the scope of this work.

Scans

Bone scan

See Nuclear Medicine section

CAT/CT: Computed axial tomography

This provides a series of "slices" via x-ray. The computer builds up pictures from the density of the tissue through which the rays pass.

Doppler

This test is to review variation in blood supply at particular parts of body. For example it will test the efficiency of blood flow through the legs.

Echocardiogram

This test is a review of actions of heart valves.

ECG: Electrocardiogram

A review of heart rate and rhythm.

EEG: Electroencephalogram

A review of brain activity.

EMG: Electromyogram

A review of nerve impulse in particular area.

Mammography

X-ray study of breast for cancer.

MRI: Magnetic Resonance Imaging

This is the application of a powerful magnetic field and use of pulses of radio waves. It can provide images which can be viewed transversely, obliquely and longitudinally.

It forms part of the radiology department.

Nuclear medicine

The use of a radioactive element which when present internally can show on film by concentrating in particular areas. This can be used to show a process at work or any abnormailities.

It is often used for liver, spleen, kidneys or lungs. It is also used for bone scans to show areas of bone growth or repair and bone cancers.

USS: Ultrasound

X-ray

Some common x-ray abbreviations include the following:–

- AXR   Abdominal
- CXR   Chest
- PXR   Pelvic

Contrast Dyes

Angiography

Investigation of the veins or arteries of a particular area. Injection of contrast medium into either veins or artery as appropriate.

Can also be known as **ARTERIOGRAPHY** or **VENOGRAPHY**

Barium enema

This is where radio opaque dye is inserted via the rectum. It is usually used to review the lower part of the bowel.

Barium meal

This is the same principle as Barium enema but concerned with the upper gastro intestinal tract.

Catheters

The insertion of dye via the artery to check a particular area of the vascular system (veins and arteries).

Cardiac catheters check the state of the blood supply for the heart.

Cholangiography

A contrast medium inserted in bile ducts. It is useful for detecting stones.

Cholescystography

The ingestion of dye which can be seen in bile from the gallbladder.

Cystogram/Urography

Dye which demonstrates flow of urine.

HSG: Hystero salpingogram

Dye is inserted via the vagina to check patency or otherwise of fallopian tubes.

IVP: Intravenous Pyelogram

Dye is inserted to check flow of urine through the kidneys and urine output.

PTC/perc: Percutaneous transhepatic cholangiography

Insertion of contrast dye/medium into the liver. This shows obstructions around the liver.

Urography

A review of bladder and ureters

Scopes: (endoscopy)

Endoscopy now usually means the use of small fibre optic instruments which are introduced into various sections of the body.

Arthroscopy

Using the scope to inspect inside a joint.

Colonoscopy

This is the inspection of the large bowel.

Colposcopy

Here the scope is inserted into vagina and cervix.

Cystourthroscopy

The review of urethra, bladder and prostate.

Duodenoscopy

The review of the duodenum.

ERCP: Endoscopic retrograde cholangio-pancreatography

The review of the bilary system.

Hysteroscopy

Scope to visualise reproductive system of woman. Enter via vagina.

Laparoscopy

Use of scope to allow visualisation of particular area, e.g., the state of ovaries and uterus for women.

Larngynogoscopy

The use of the scope to review larynx.

OGD: Oesophageal gastro-duodenoscopy

Also known as gastroscopy, this is using the scope to review the stomach and first part of the bowel.

Sigmoidoscopy

The scope is inserted via the rectum to review the final part of the bowel and the rectum.

Proctoscopy

The scope is inserted via the rectum to inspect and examine the internal part of the rectum.

Other Tests

LP Lumbar puncture

Insertion of a needle into spinal canal to take fluid, inject contrast dyes. This is often used as a test for meningitis. It is now being superceded by more advanced tests for certain conditions.

Biopsies

The selection of sections of tissue to review cells. It is usually taken under local anaesthetic.

Aspirations

The removal of fluid for further microbiological review, for example, bone marrow aspiration is to show up abnormalities of bone marrow. The fluid is taken from the hip or breast bone usually.

Audiometry

This is the assessment of hearing and ability to distinguish sounds at dfferent pitches and volumes.

Tympanometry

This measures the resistance of pressure in the ears which helps to determine the cause of hearing loss.

Skin allergy tests

Usually taken on arm or back this tests minute sections of skin against various possible allergens.

Gynaecology and Obstetric tests

CTG: Cardiotopography

Used to trace the fetal heart against contractions (if present).

FBS: Fetal blood sample

A small amount of blood is taken from the fetal scalp – to test for pH. It indicates whether the fetus is in distress.

Amniocentesis

A specimen of fluid is taken from around the sac surrounding the baby while in the uterus. It is to test for genetic disorders.

Chorionic Villus Sampling (CVS)

A sample of fluid is taken from the placenta to test for genetic disorders.

Chromosomal Specimen

Blood sampling used for genetic disease or sex determination.

Papanicolaou Smear (pap)

Smear testing for identification of abnormal cells in cervix or sexually transmitted disease.

Examinations

Cranial nerves – **see** Neurology sections
Reflexes – **see** Neurology section
Muscle weakness – **see** Orthopaedic section
Child development – **see** Paediatrics
Foetal development – **see** Obstetrics
Cardiac examination – **see** relevant section

Pulmonary/Respiratory tests

Most respiratory tests involve breathing or exhaling at some force into equipment. The most simple is the peak flow used on the wards routinely.

Other tests and significance

Description	Name	Normal range
Air left in lung after deep Exhalation	Residual volume RV	1200 ml
Air left after normal exhalation	Functional residual capacity FRC	2400 ml
Air exhaled after deep exhalation	Vital capacity VC	4800 ml
Usual amount of air inhaled or exhaled	Tidal volume TV	5–10 ml/kg weight
Total air in lungs (inhaling)	Total Lung capacity TLC	6000 ml

Medications

Medications

Medications and prescriptions

Review of records

It is beyond the scope of this book to provide a detailed review of all medications and usages. An updated formulary or the *Data Sheet compendium* should be used in practice. However there are certain common themes to reviewing prescriptions and to working out their significance or effect.

The following is a reasonable method of reviewing prescription records:

A. *Type of medication prescribed*

(**See** table 1 below)
Is it appropriate for the problem?

B. *Dosage*

Dosage will vary according to age, in some cases size (particularly in children). Anaesthetic medication should always be considered against the size and weight of the individual. The assumption that the patient is an average sized adult is often incorrect.

C. Method of administration

Table 1

Abbreviation	Meaning
PO	Oral
SC	Sub cutaneous injection
IM	Intra muscular injection
IV	Intra venous injection
IVI	Intravenous infusion
PV	By vagina (per vaginum)
PR	By rectum (per rectum)
Local/topical	Applied to skin
SL	Under the tongue (sub lingual)
Drops	Into eye or ear
By nebuliser	By use of nebuliser – allows medication to be given through oxygen mask
ID	Intra dermal*
IT	Intra thecal*
Deep IM	Deep intra muscular
Depot	Long term deep Intramuscular injection usually used for psychiatric medications

---

* Rarely used
Intravenous medications – can be provided in ampoule form or can be in the form of dry powder, which is reconstituted with either Water for Injections or Sodium Chloride. Care should be taken to ensure correct fluid is used when reconstituting powder (see I)

D. Timing of medication

Table 2

Abbreviation		Meaning
OD		Once a day
BD	/bid*	Twice a day
TDS	/tid*	Three times a day
QDS	/qid*	Four times a day
Nocte		At night
Mane		In the morning
PRN		As needed
Pre med		Pre surgery (usually one hour before)
4 hly		Four hourly
OM		Once in morning
OE		Once in evening
Alt die		Alternative days
Alt nocte		Alternative nights

*older abbreviations. Now rarely used.

E. Side effects

What types are common?

F. Patient allergies

Are these likely to be affected. Has the patient had an allergic reaction to this type of drug before?

G. Interactions

Are they allowed to be given together? Many drugs are not.

H. Vulnerable patients

The elderly, children, pregnant women and those with immune problems are types of vulnerable patient – can the drug be prescribed for these groups?

I. If in intravenous infusion or needing to be added to fluid

Many drugs will not work with particular fluids or drugs. Check compatibility and which fluids used.

J. TTO/TTA – to take out/to take away – medications on discharge

Can the patient use them? Explanation of use and ability to understand or use properly.

K. Given by the appropriate individual

Most health care trusts will restrict staff that can give intravenous injections or set up infusions with medications added. Cytotoxic drugs are also often restricted. Did the member of staff have the authority or training to give the medication?

L. Children's dosages

Usually health care trusts will require nurses to take some form of mathematical assessment before calculating children's dosages. Medical staff often express paediatric dosages as an amount or weight.

Infusions and Incompatibility

Drug	Infusion	Issues	Incompatibility
Ampicillin	Sodium chloride	Fine	
As above	Dextrose/Sodium lactate	Unstable – reduced efficacy	
Aminophylline			Erthromycin Cephalosporins Tetracycline Penicillins Hydrocortisone
Calcium Gluconate			Magnesium Sulphate
Calcium Salts			Tetracyclines
Cephalosporins	Sodium Chloride fluid	Do not add	Gentamicin Aminophylline Tetracyclines Erthromycin Heparin Hydrocortisone
Chloramphenicol			Erthromycin Tetracyclines Hydrocortisone
Gentamicin	Never as IVI. Never mix with penicillins	Bolus injection	Penicillins Cephalosporins Heparin
Erthromycin	Reconstitute first with water for injections before adding to any infusion	All infusion fluids ok	
Heparin			Erthromycin Gentamicin Hydrocortisone Tetracyclines Penicillin Cephalosporins
Hydrocortisone			Heparin Aminophylline Chloramphenicol Penicillin Cephalosporins

Drug	Infusion	Issues	Incompatibility
Magnesium Sulphate			Tetracycline Calcium gluconate
Penicillins			Gentamicin Aminophylline Erthromycin Heparin Hydrocortisone Tetracyclines
Tetracycline	Water for injection for reconstitution	Care with rate of infusion (Control carefully)	Aminophylline Calcium salts Magnesium salts Heparin Erthromycin Cephalosporins Penicillin Chloramphenicol
Chlorpromazine	Preferably IM. Sodium chloride should be used	NO other drugs added	
Diazepam	All infusion fluids but slow bolus* dose preferred	NO other drugs added	
Frusemide	Sodium chloride/ Hartmanns	NO other drugs added	
Hydrocortisone	Reconstitute with water for injections then added to fluids	Fine	
Isoprenaline	5% dextrose	Never bolus dose	
Potassium chloride	Dilute to specific requirements. Care with maximum dose/weight – even in adults	All fluids	

*bolus – once off loading dose.

Types of Medications

Summary of types of Medications

Medications	Use	Side effects	Extra notes	Other drugs which may react
Analgesics	Pain relief	Gastrointestinal tract upset	See specifics	
Antibiotics	Infection	Nausea vomiting	See specific details	
Anti coagulant	Increase time for clotting of blood	Bleeding	Blood levels need to be monitored often	Aspirin
Anti convulsants	Stop/reduce fits	Drowsiness	Depends on type fit/brain site	Tricyclic anti depressants Lignocaine
Anti cholinergic	Relaxes muscles, reduces tremor	Dry mouth, blurred vision	Caution with patient with glaucoma	
Anti depressants	Avoid depression	Drowsiness Lethargy	See specifics	
Anti emetics	Prevent vomiting – some used for anxiety, vertigo	Depends on which used. Can lead to drowsiness	Caution with liver, kidney and heart failure	Large number of medications including hypoglycaemics and amphetamine
Anti fibrinolytic	Helps prevent clots	Bleeding	Caution with liver and kidney	Anti coagulants
Anti histamines	Reduces effect of allergy	Blurred vision gastric upset and drowsiness	Sedative effect can be problem	
Anti hypertensive	Reduces blood pressure	Rash, gastric irritation, sudden drop in BP	Care with diuretics	Non Potassium Sparing diuretics

Medications	Use	Side effects	Extra notes	Other drugs which may react
Barbituates	Sleep, anaesthetic & anti convulsants	Gastro intestinal upset	Care because depresses respiratory funcion (not to be given to patients with respiratory problems) Dependency and addiction issues	Alcohol – exacerbates
Beta Blockers	Cardiac and anxiety	Drowsiness, gastric upset, dizziness	Care with diabetics – difficulty in recognising diabetic problems	
Corticosteroids	Inflammation	Mask symptoms	See specific section	
Hypo-glycaemics	Control blood sugar	Inconsistent blood sugar levels	Needs monitoring	Care with NSAID
Laxatives	Reduce constipation	Diarrhoea		Variety of forms
Non steroidal anti inflammatory drugs (NSAID)	Reduce inflammation – particularly effective in arthritic conditions	Gastric upset, gastric bleeding, vomiting and diarrhoea	Care with patients with peptic ulcer, asthma (some are hypersensitive), liver or kidney damage	Care with warfarin (tends to increase effectiveness) and oral hypoglycaemic medication
Neuroleptics	Sedative, calming effect	Gastric upset, drowsiness, dermatitis in some, postural hypotension (Blood pressure fall when stand up)	Care where low blood pressure Irreversible side effects tardive dyskinesia	See detailed later

Medications	Use	Side effects	Extra notes	Other drugs which may react
Cardiac glycosides	Reduces arrhythmias Slows and makes more effective use of heart beat	Gastric upset. Confusion, diarrhoea, loss of appetite	Side effects may mean dose too high. Contraindicated with certain arrhythmias including Wolff Parkinson white syndrome Also in some forms of cardio-myopathy	Care with Amiodarone Quinidine Diuretics Spironalactone Verapamil
Diuretics	Use for fluid retention	Excessive fluid loss Problems with electrolyte disturbance	Monitor electrolyte levels	

Medications: Specific categories

Specific categories of medications include:

- Analgesics
- Antibiotics
- Anticoagulants
- Anti convulsants
- Anti depressants
- Cardiac Medications
- Corticosteroids
- Hypoglycaemics

Analgesics

Types –

1. Common analgesics
2. Non steroid anti inflammatory drugs
3. Narcotics
4. Intravenous narcotics

There are a number of different types of analgesics, some of which have additional uses.

1. *Common analgesics include:*

A. Paracetamol

Paracetamol can be used for pain relief and a side effect can be reduction of temperature. Children's varieties are available.

Paracetamol are useful for those who have suffered gastric problems and require mild analgesia. If taken in large dosage they can result in irreversible liver damage. There is a regime for treatment of overdose but much depends on the speed by which it is commenced.

B. Aspirin

Aspirin reduces pain and inflammation. They are also useful as a means of reducing clotting and helping in heart conditions.

They should be given with great caution to children under seven.

2. *NSAID – Non steroidal anti inflammatory drugs*

NSAIDs also have an analgesic effect. There are a wide variety of medications from various sources.

Types –

- anthranilic acid derivatives –
  e.g.: Mefenamic acid etc
- Indole acetic derivatives –
  e.g.: Indomethacin etc
- Salicylates
  e.g.: Aspirin
- Phenylacetic derivatives
  e.g.: Diclofenac

- Pyrazoles:
  e.g.: Asapropazone
- Propionic acid derivatives:
  e.g.: Ibuprofen
- Others:
  e.g.: Piroxicam

Frequent side effects and problems

Side effects and problems include gastro intestinal upsets such as loss of appetite, nausea, vomiting, diarrhoea, and gastric bleeding.

Conditions to check

Condition	Problem	Use
Renal (kidney) failure	Accumulates in kidney and can have toxic effects	Limited – dose as low as possible
Liver failure	Can lead to nephritis (inflammation of the liver). Toxic levels can accumulate in liver	Limited – dose as low as possible
Asthma	Can precipitate broncho spasm (spasm of the bronchi of the lungs leading to breathing problems)	Contra indicated
Peptic ulceration – past or current history	Can lead to gastric bleeding and upset – exacerbate original condition	Contra indicated
Pregnancy	May appear in breast milk	Do not use if possible
Cardiac problems	Can lead to retention of salt and water which can exacerbate cardiac failure and increase blood pressure	Restrict use – not all have this effect

3. Narcotics

Narcotics vary in their strength and affect but on the whole they are powerful analgesic drugs, which have a direct effect on the central nervous system.

In some cases the drugs are also used as pre-medications to relax patients prior to surgery. Their use is largely controlled. Paediatric dosages are available.

Types include:
- Codeine
- Dihydrocodeine
- Pethidine
- Papaveretum
- Dextromoromide
- Methadone
- Morphine
- Diamorphine

Method of administration:
- Oral – immediate effect
- Oral – slow release (over period of hours)
- Sub cutaneous injection with some
- Intra muscular injection
- Intravenous injection
- Intravenous infusion

Side effects and problems:
The common side effect is nausea, therefore many are given routinely with anti-emetics to prevent nausea, addiction and constipation.

Table of side effects and problems

Condition	Problem	Use
Respiratory conditions	Respiratory depressants (stop the respiratory system working effectively sedative effect	Great care with these groups of patients. Particularly in injection form. Not to use unless absolutely necessary where patient has chronic obstructive airways
On anti depressants – MAOIs	Combination of both sets of drugs can cause serve cardiac problems	No use while on MAOIs. Not within 2 weeks of withdrawal
Renal (kidney) failure	Accumulates in kidney and can have toxic effects	Limited – dose as low as possible
Liver cirrhosis	Increases sedation	Limited – dose as low as possible
Raised intra cranial pressure (Pressure inside skull has increased) and head injuries	Masks symptoms Increases sedation	Limited – great care
Pregnancy	Can have sedative effect on foetus. Crosses placenta and breast milk	Care needed

4. *Intravenous Narcotics*

These are the better-known medications and subject certainly within hospitals to significant controls. Usually given with anti-emetics because of the nausea they induce. Some types have an anti-emetic within the medication (Cylimorph). Side effects are as above. See also section on Infusion Fluids.

Antibiotics

Anti-biotic, anti-microbial (destroy microbes) and amino glycosides (destroy particular types of bacteria) are often all classed as antibiotics.

Antibiotics combat bacteria and can be either broad or narrow spectrum depending on the type and bacteria concerned.

Broad-spectrum antibiotics

Broad-spectrum antibiotics are useful in dealing with a number of infections but increasingly the medical profession is aware of the risks of over use. Some "super" bacteria – resistant to a number of antibiotics are now developing and treating those infections is becoming a problem.

Narrow-spectrum antibiotics

Narrow-spectrum antibiotics are more specific to particular types of bacteria and are generally more effective.

Side effects and Problems

Antibiotics do have side effects, including, but not limited to, nausea, vomiting, and headaches, and, in severe cases anaphylactic shock (an extreme allergic reaction causing possible respiratory distress or death). For this reason allergies should be checked carefully before antibiotics are given.

There are a substantial number of antibiotics now but they fall into specific groupings including the penicillin, erythromycin (for those allergic to penicillin) and flagyl groups. Since they are effective on different bacteria they are used for different conditions. In many cases after 48 hours an improvement should be noticeable. All courses should be completed.

Antibiotic	General use	Issues and problems	Method of administration
Penicillin based (amoxycillin, ampicillin, flucloxicillin)	Broad spectrum Streptococci infections Some bacilli infections Respiratory tract infection, urinary tract and gynaecological infections	Penicillin allergy can be severe and fatal. Side effects – diarrhoea, rash, vomiting, gastric upset	Most oral, IM and IV IM injections usually painful
Cephalosporins Such as velosef and cephradine	Broad spectrum Staphylococci, some forms streptococci and E Coli in large doses Respiratory tract, urinary tract, skin and gastro intestinal tract infections	Partial cross allergy with those allergic to penicillin Side effects – gastro intestinal usually where allergies pre exist such as asthmatics	Oral, IM and IV
Aminoglycosides Such as gentamicin, Amikacin and Tobramycin	Severe infection from Gram negative source Used when other antibiotics likely to be ineffective	Severe side effects including hearing problems Needs care with kidney damage	Only in injection form
Sulphonamides Such as Trimethoprim Co-trimazole	Useful for some forms of pneumonia especially in AIDS patients, toxoplasmosis (affects foetus) and urinary infections	Usual gastric upsets and rashes. Joint pains and loss of appetite. Care with liver or kidney disease Interacts with certain medications particularly anti coagulants and anti convulsants	Oral, syrup and tablet, and for intravenous infusion

Antibiotic	General use	Issues and problems	Method of administration
Macrolides – Such as Erythromycin	Respiratory and gastric infections Also chlamydia	Gastric upsets, abdominal pain and reversible hearing loss Interacts with number of other medications	Oral, gel for topical application and intravenous infusion
Quinolones such as Ciprofloxacin	Respiratory, urinary, gastric infections. Also skin infections	Local irritation with eye drops Gastric upsets, sleep disturbance, anxiety, sensitivity to light and joint and muscle aches Interacts with large number of medications	Oral, eye drops and intravenous infusion
Others – Metronidazole (flagyl)	Gastric and genito urinary infection, general surgery	Gastric upsets, rashes, swelling of face, drowsiness, headaches and epileptic seizures on prolonged therapy. Avoid alcohol. Caution with pregnancy	Gel, cream, suppositories, oral, intravenous
Vancomycin	Endocarditis and serious infections. Infection of large bowel	Kidney damage and tinnitus in large doses. Blood disorders, fever, low blood pressure Avoid rapid infusion Urine and blood tests for kidney function throughout. Can react with other antibiotics	Usually IV Occasionally oral
Tetracycline	Sexually transmitted disease Respiratory and genital infections	Gastric upset, visual disturbance. Rash-discontinue. Discolour bones and exacerbate kidney failure Reacts with different medications	Oral or topical

Anti-coagulants

These are medications which aim to prevent blood clots. This is achieved usually by inhibiting clotting factors from forming. The normal pattern is for a loading or higher dose to be given at the beginning of treatment. Following this the level of drug is measured regularly by blood tests. The dosage of medication can be varied according to the blood levels maintaining the optimum level in the blood system.

Some conditions will affect the level of anti-coagulant in the blood such as infection, weight loss or, other medications. Anticoagulants are usually only prescribed if essential. Caution is particularly required if a person has kidney or liver problems or it has proved impossible to control the blood pressure.

There are also times when the use of anti-coagulants is unhelpful, such as after labour or surgery when the risk of haemorrhage is higher in any event.

Usual Types

There are two usual types although aspirin can also be used as long-term management:

- Warfarin (Tablet form) long-term management
- Heparin (sub cutaneous injection) acute management of thrombosis or emboli, prevention of same when on bed rest for period of time.

Interactions with other medications

The following can increase the effect of warfarin:

- Anabolic steroids
- Analgesics – co proximal, Paracetamol and Aspirin
- Anti arrhythmias – Amiodarone
- Antibiotics such as Erythromycin and Metronidazole
- Anti depressants such as Amitryptline and the SSRIs
- Corticosteroids
- Non-Steroid anti-inflammatory drugs
- Some hormones such as testosterone

The effectiveness of Warfarin can be reduced by

- Vitamin K
- Oral contraceptive pill
- Anti epileptics – Carbemazepine and Phenobarbitone

The following can increase the effect of Heparin:

- Aspirin
- Dipyridamole
- Non steroid anti inflammatory drugs such as Diclofenac – increase risk of gastric bleeding

The following may decrease the effect of Heparin

- GTN glyceryl trinitrate (cardiac)

Anti-convulsants

These are medications, which control epilepsy. Epilepsy itself is not one condition but a group of chronic conditions, which can be categorised according to the types of fit or area of the brain affected.

Usually anti-convulsant medication needs to be taken for life, although this may be in small dosages. Medication should not be stopped suddenly for any reason. They can also be affected by other medications such as particular types of anti-depressants (tricyclics) and lignocaine (local anaesthetic). This can make them much less effective. In some cases the use of anti-convulsants can render other medications less effective such as oral contraceptives and anti-coagulants (designed to prevent clotting of the blood).

Anti-depressants and anti-psychotics

These fall into a number of categories:

- Benzodiazepines
- Phenothiazines
- Other anti-psychotics
- MAOIs
- Tricyclics

- SSRIs
- Others:

Benzodiapines

To some extent this medication is discredited now because of the addiction issues and litigation. As anti-depressants these medications should generally only be used for short periods (four weeks). Modern anti-depressants are usually considered more effective and have less side effects. Benzodiapines are more likely to be used as sedatives (such as pre-medication or sleeping tablets).

They are usually given in tablet form or as syrup via infusions and via the rectum. The most commonly used is Diazepam (Valium). This is used for a variety of differing purposes:

Problems and Conditions

Condition	Problem	Issues
Pulmonary insufficiency and respiratory depression	In IV form in particular some risk of depressing the respiratory system so that it is less effective. Where there are also problems with the system this can have serious consequences	Contra indicated in acute pulmonary insufficiency and respiratory depression
Psychological conditions	Exacerbates phobic and obsessional conditions. Also chronic psychoses	Contra indicated. In some patients hallucinations can also occur
Depression	Can precipitate suicide	Not to be used on own for depression. More effective against anxiety problems
Pregnancy	Can Pass via breast milk High doses in 3rd trimester (Third) of pregnancy reported to produce foetal hert rate irregularities, with poor sucking in neonate	Avoid if possible

There are a large number of benzodiazepines and some have more helpful uses:

- Nitrazepam, Triazolam and Temazepam – sedatives – used as sleeping tablets
- Clonazepam – anti convulsants
- Chlordiazepoxide – control of DTs in alcohol patients
- Diazepam – Muscular spasms and pre-medication

Phenothiazines

These are also a wide variety of drugs with a number of purposes. The most notable purpose however is their ability to act as significant tranquillisers. They are often associated with psychiatric inpatient care because of their ability to control the behaviour of disturbed patients.

Examples are:

- Chlorpromazine (largactyl)
- Prochlorperazine
- Promazine

Most come in a variety of forms including tablets, syrup and for injection. If they are given by injection a deep intramuscular injection must be used. Most are irrititants and cannot be given via a sub-cutaneous route.

Indications for use include
- Schizophrenia and other psychoses, mania
- Acute anxiety and agitation disorders
- Intractable hiccups

In the past they have been used where other medications have failed to prevent nausea in the terminally ill.

Problems and side effects

Condition	Problem	Issues
Neurological conditions	Well known side effects include the development of TARDIVE DYSKINESIA Involuntary movements Parkinsonian type symptoms can also develop	In some cases other medications have to be provided to reduce symptoms. Where phenothiazines given for long time or large dose – check what other medications have been prescribed
Liver	Jaundice can develop in small numbers of patients	Contra indicated in patients with liver problems
Kidney	Kidney failure or dysfunction (problems with function)	Contra indicated
Cardiac	Can cause increased heart rate (tachycardia) and arrhythmias some of a serious nature (VT and VF) (see cardiac section) Can also cause postural hypotension Fall in blood pressure on change of position – standing usually	Contra indicated where history of cardiac failure. Care with other cardiac patients Often given infusions of some phenothiazines while patient lying down and blood pressure being monitored
Eye	Changes in the eye can occur with some	Contra indicated where narrow angle glaucoma present
Skin	Irritant	Skin rashes where in contact. Photosensitivity may develop in large or long-term use
Pregnancy	May prolong labour Passes via breast milk	Only if necessary

Interaction with other medication

Phenothiazines may interact with other medications making them less effective or exacerbating their effect:

- Anti-cholinergic medication – may be enhanced while anti-cholinergic medication itself may reduce the anti-psychotic effect of some phenothiazines
- Sedatives – can exacerbate the sedative effect of phenothiazines, particularly a problem where respiratory difficulties
- Anti-hypertensives to reduce blood pressure – can have increased effect
- Hypoglycaemic agents designed to keep blood sugar levels under control may have less effect
- Some medications work against phenothiazines – for example adrenaline, amphetamine and levodopa.
- Lithium may reduce the ability to absorb phenothiazines, as can some anti parkinsonian drugs

Other anti-psychotics

Include the following:

- Butyrophenones – Haloperidol, Droperidol
- Thioxanthenes – Flupenthixol
- Others – Loxapine

Otherwise known as the major tranquillisers (Neuroleptic medications) their short term use is to control aggressive, disturbed or agitated patients, who show acute symptoms of mania and schizophrenia. They are used for the long term management of schizophrenia.

Their side effects can be similar as above depending on the medication used.

Interaction with other medication

- Amiodarone – arrhythmias
- Anaesthetics – lowers blood pressure
- Other anti depressants
- Anti histamines – can cause cardiac arrhythmias
- Sedatives – enhanced effect

MAOIs – monoamine oxidase inhibitors

MAOIs work on brain enzymes. They can interact (often quite dangerously) with certain foods, beverages and medications. They are less often used. They are used for people who may not respond to tricyclics and are often the last choice.

They include the following:

- Isocarboxazid
- Phenelzine
- Tranylcypromine * most dangerous
- Moclobemide

Side effects

- Sudden fall in blood pressure on standing
- Drowsiness
- Gastric disturbances
- Headache
- Weight gain
- Mania

Precautions

Patients on these medications should avoid food rich in tyramine such as cheese, meats, yeast extracts, herrings and wine, as the combination can lead to a severe and dangerous rise in blood pressure.

Interactions with other medication

- Opiates – can cause severe reactions
- Anti depressants –
- Anti hypertensives – enhanced effect in lowering blood pressure
- Levodopa – dangerous rise in blood pressure
- Carbemazepine – increased risk of convulsions
- Sympathomimetics – dangerous rise in blood pressure
  1. Dopamine
  2. Dexamphetamine
  3. Methylphenidate
  4. Pemoline
  5. Ephedrine
     (Many of which are present in cough mixtures and decongestants)

Tricyclics

In common use. Precise mechanism is not understood. Can have marked sedative qualities. Takes a number of weeks before they have effect – buld up of certain levels before effective.

Examples:

- Amitriptyline
- Doxepin
- Timipramine
- Dothiepin

Caution with patients prone to seizures – can lower the threshold and make fit more easily. To avoid in epileptics if possible.

Side effects – dry mouth, blurred vision, constipation and rapid heart beat. Also can cause gastrointestinal upsets. Large doses can be dangerous to the cardiac system.

SSRIs – Selective serotonin reuptake inhibitors

SSRIs have a less sedative effect than tricyclics. They have fewer side effects which are blurred vision, dry mouth and more gastro-intestinal effects. These are the newer medications and often used.

They include the following:

- Citaloprim
- Fluoxetine
- Fluvoxamine maleate
- Paroxetine
- Sertaline

Precautions
Care should be taken for patients suffering from liver, kidney or heart disease, epilepsy, pregnancy, and also patients undergoing electro-convulsive therapy.

Interaction with other medication
- Anti coagulants – increased effects on anti-coagulants
- Anti epileptics – increase risk of convulsion
- Lithium – increase toxic effects
- MAOIs – increased effect

Cardiac Medications

Diuretics

These drugs act on the kidneys to increase the excretion of water from the system. Different diuretics act specifically on differing parts of the kidneys. Some such as frusemide (Lasix) will also result in the removal of valuable electrolytes such as potassium. Removal or reduction of important electrolytes can result in cardiac problems.

Some diuretics will lead to kidney failure if used with particular types of antibiotics.

Diuretics can be given intravenously, intramuscularly or via tablets/syrups.

Beta-blockers

Part of the nervous system works by affecting specific sites within the body known as beta adrenoreceptors. Without providing a lengthy and detailed review of how this system works beta adrenoreceptors have an effect on either the cardiac system (by increasing cardiac output) or on the lungs (by dilating the smaller bronchioles in the lungs). It depends on the type of beta-receptor as to which system will be affected.

The use of beta-blockers has probably increased in recent years but they are mainly used for prevention of angina, managing high blood pressure or controlling abnormal heart rhythms.

Side effects

Side effects include a slowing of the heart rate, some gastric problems such as nausea and vomiting, and problems of the central nervous system such as dizziness or hallucination. Care needs to be taken if they are prescribed for diabetics and in some patients heart failure will develop.

Although there are a number of brand names, any medication which ends in olol, is often a beta-blocker.

Cardiac Glycosides

These are used in the treatment of congestive cardiac failure and control heart rhythm problems.

Most common used is DIGOXIN which has been developed from the foxglove plant.

Side effects are common so care with monitoring side effects must be taken.

Side effects

- nausea
- vomiting
- loss of appetite
- confusion
- arrhythmias

Cardiac glycosides can interact with other medication, including:

- Amiodarone
- Diuretics
- Quinidine
- Spironolactone
- Verapamil
  (Often also prescribed to cardiac patients particularly the Amiodarone and diuretics)

Contra indications include the following

- intermittent heart block
- Supraventricular arrhythmias such as Wolff Parkinson White syndrome
- Hypertrophic cardiomyopathy (see cardiac section).

Precautions

Care is needed with the following:

- Thyroid patients
- The elderly
- Pregnancy (although no particular risk)
- Severe respiratory disease

Administration

- Oral – tablets
- Oral – syrup
- Infusion – IM route painful use IV

Anti-angina medication

These are medications, which strictly speaking are not placed within a specific group but have the same purpose – to prevent angina and chest pain. The most notable is that of GTN (glycerol trinitrate). The mechanism by which this medication works is beyond the scope of this book but its effect is to dilate the blood vessels reducing the volume of blood, which returns to the right side of the heart. This allows a temporary reduction in the amount of work the heart undertakes and reduces pressure on the heart.

In some people there are side effects of dizziness or fainting but for many it is an effective way of preventing an angina attack. It can be taken sublingually (under the tongue) or at regular times by slow release tablets.

Anti-arrhythmias

There are a variety of medications that control arrhythmias including some in the former mentioned categories. The most common used medication is probably still AMIODARONE. Others are Quidinine, Flecainide, and Disopyramide.

These medications slow down the nerve impulses to the heart and are used for the more life threatening arrhythmias such as the ventricular problems. They have potentially serious side effects and are therefore used initially at least under close medical supervision.

Side effects

- Increased sensitivity to sunlight
- Impairment of vision – ophthalmic checks required when problems develop
- Peripheral neuropathy (disease or deterioration in the peripheral nervous system (limbs)
- Thyroid problems

Precautions

Care is needed with:

- Patients in sinus bradycardia (slow but regular heart beat)
- Cardiac failure, which has not been controlled
- On beta blockers
- With thyroid disease
- Digoxin

Interactions with medications

Amiodarone, in particular, interacts with a number of different medications, which can result in serious ventricular arrhythmias.

- Other anti arrhythmic drugs
- Antibiotics – Erythromycin or Co trimoxazole
- Anti coagulants
- Ant histamines
- Anti malarials
- Anti psychotics – phenothazines, haloperidol
- Beta-blockers
- Digoxin
- Anti-convulsants – phenytoin
- Tricyclic anti depressants

Ace Inhibitors (Angiotension converting enzyme inhibitors)

These are being used increasingly following heart attacks, in cardiac failure, to control blood pressure and in diabetes. There are many types and there generally end in -pril.

Side effects

- low blood pressure
- kidney failure
- cough

Interactions

- They can cause a high potassium depletion if given with some diuretics
- Can cause kidney failure if given with some pain killers

Contra-indications

- They should not be used in pregnancy or young women who may become pregnant

Statins

These drugs such as simvastatin, atorvastatin and pravastatin are being used increasingly in heart and stroke patients. They lower the cholesterol and may prevent future heart attacks and strokes.

Side effects

- Can cause muscle damage

Corticosteroids

These are mainly synthetic substances derived from hormones produced by the adrenal glands. Corticosteroids have two major effects:

a. Glucocorticoid resulting in an anti inflammatory response
   Useful in the treatment of rheumatic disease, inflammatory bowel disease and asthma

b. Mineralcorticoid
   Number of effects including salt and water retention

Problems and side effects

a. The most important issue with steroid usage is that they suppress the ability of the adrenal glands to produce hydrocortisone naturally. The body produces steroids naturally in response to stress, infection or injury. It may be necessary to increase the dosage at times of stress or illness. Cortico Steroids must NOT be discontinued suddenly.

b. Cushingoid syndrome
Moon face, obesity and acne

c. Electrolyte imbalance

- Salt and water retention with hypertension (increasing blood pressure)
- Reduced levels of potassium leading to muscle weakness
- Altered glucose metabolism – increased risk of developing diabetes
- Altered calcium and phosphorus balance, which may lead to osteoporosis and more fractures of the bones.

d. Depression and Psychosis
Rare but can be extreme

e. Wound healing is delayed significantly

f. Increased risk of cataracts and corneal ulcers

g. Gastric upsets.

Examples

- Beclamethasone
- Dexamethasone
- Methyprednisolone
- Prednisolone
- Hydrocortisone

Administration

Usually oral, by injection, by infusion and topical (gels etc)
Tablets are often coated (enteric coated (EC)) to prevent gastric irritation.

Interaction with other medications

(See Infusion Charts)

- Anti diabetic medication – effectiveness can be reduced
- Anti epileptic medication – effectiveness of steroids can be reduced
- Digoxin – Increasing risk of toxic effects
- Duiretics – increased loss of potassium – may require supplements

Oral Hypoglycaemics

This is medication that controls diabetes administered by tablet and diet.

Diabetes can also require controlling by injections of insulin

Types

Two main types of oral hypoglycaemics:

- Sulphonylureas and
- Biguanides

Sulphonylureas	Biguanides
Most common: GLICLAZIDE	Most common: METFORMIN
Caution – obese patients Tendency to hypoglycaemia in early hours of morning – dose to be checked carefully	**Caution** – probably drugs of choice Can alter blood biochemistry seriously – dose need to be carefully checked
Side effects: gastric upset Skin rash Blood disorders Facial flushing Sweating Breathlessness	**Side effects:** gastric upset Skin rash Muscle weakness Metallic taste
Interactions Beta Blockers – dangerous Corticosteroids may need increase Hypoglycaemic dose Diuretics: may need alter dose Alcohol: may produce hypoglycaemia MAOIs: enhance effect hypoglycaemics Salicylates: may require alter dose	**Interactions** Beta Blockers – dangerous Corticosteroids may need increase dose of hypoglycaemics Diuretics: may need alter dose Alcohol: may produce hypoglycaemia MAOIs: enhance effect of hypoglycaemics Salicylates: may require alter dose

Cardiac System

Cardiac System

Anatomy and Physiology

The heart is made of three layers of tissue:

a.   Pericardium
b.   Myocardium
c.   Endocardium

Pericardium

The pericardium is made of two sacs. The outer sac is made of fibrous tissue and prevents the heart becoming distended.

The inner layer, which is made of a double layer of membrane, is attached to the heart muscle. The membrane secretes fluid in between the layers of membrane to ensure movement between the layers.

Myocardium

The myocardium is the middle layer of tissue. It consists of special muscle with the appearance of a sheet of muscle. As an impulse of contraction commences it can spread throughout the layer.

Endocardium

This is essentially the lining of the myocardium similar in constituents as the lining of blood vessels, which enter the heart.

Structure of the Heart

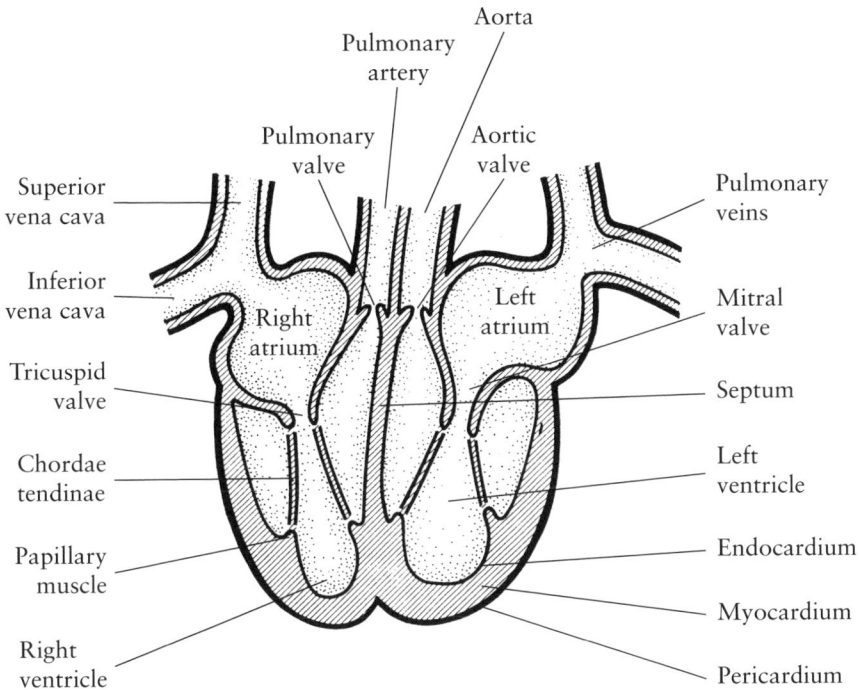

Aorta

Pulmonary
artery

Pulmonary
valve

Aortic
valve

Superior
vena cava

Pulmonary
veins

Inferior
vena cava

Right
atrium

Left
atrium

Mitral
valve

Tricuspid
valve

Septum

Chordae
tendinae

Left
ventricle

Papillary
muscle

Endocardium

Right
ventricle

Myocardium

Pericardium

The heart is divided into two sides and four chambers. The right side of the heart contains blood, which has reduced oxygen. The blood comes from the rest of the body and is on its way to the lungs to pick up further oxygen for transporting to the body. This process is also a means of removing carbon dioxide from the blood supply.

Blood enters via either the *Superior Vena Cava* or the *Inferior Vena Cava*. These are two substantial blood vessels carrying blood directly back to the heart.

The blood passes from the first chamber (the right atrium) through to the lower chamber (right ventricle) through the *tricuspid valve*, which restricts and controls the amount of blood travelling between the two chambers.

From the right ventricle blood passes through to the *right and left pulmonary arteries* to the lungs. In the lungs blood collects oxygen and returns to the left side of the heart via the *pulmonary veins*. The left side of the heart contains oxygenated blood. The blood, newly oxygenated, passes into the left atrium from where it passes through the *Mitral valve* into the left ventricle. The mitral valve, like the other valves in the heart, controls the flow of blood between sections ensuring that an adequate amount passes through on each contraction.

The left ventricle is the pump of the heart in the sense that its primary task is to force the oxygenated blood out of the heart into the circulatory system and the rest of the body. The blood is forced into the *aorta*, which is the largest and most important artery in the body. The aorta will then distribute the blood around the system, supplying oxygen as it travels.

Conduction

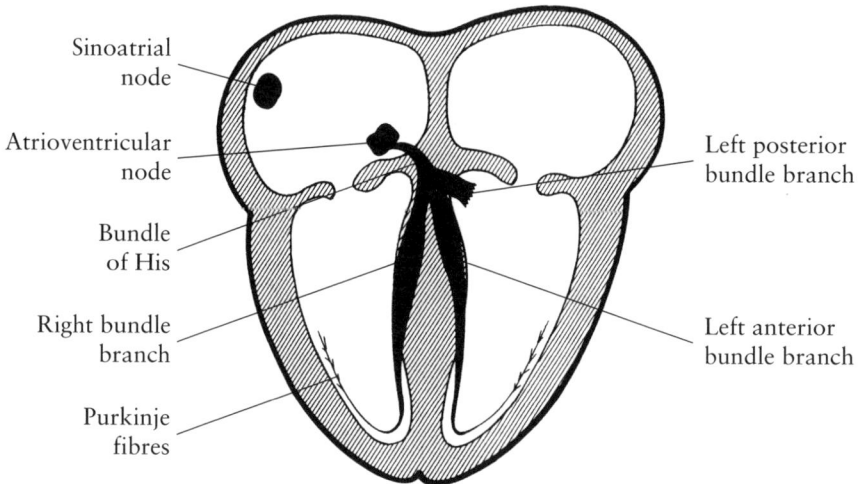

The heart, when performing as a pump, needs a current of some kind to force the various parts to contract or dilate and ensure blood is moved around the system as needed.

The cells for the conduction are placed within the myocardium, the middle layer of the heart. The mechanism works by two nodes (central areas of cells which initiate movement). The first and most important is that of the *Sino Atrial node* which is placed in the right atrium. Known as the pacemaker, its primary function is to initiate the movement of cardiac cells. It forces the surrounding cells to form a contraction movement, which forces the blood into the right ventricle.

There is a further node placed near the tricuspid valve and is usually stimulated by the contraction of the myocardium started by the SA node. This is known as the *Atrio Ventricular node* (AV Node).

However, if needed, the AV node can also stimulate activity albeit at a slower rate.

The Atrioventricular bundle/Bundle of His

These are fibres, which convey the conduction throughout to other parts of the heart. They are connected to the AV Node and divide into right and left just below the node where the ventricles are separated by the *Septum*. When the fibres reach the ventricle part of the heart they further divide into fine specialist fibres within the myocardium. These are the *Purkinje fibres* and their role is to transmit the waves of contraction through to the rest of the heart.

Nerve supply

The heart can also be affected by the nervous system. Without detailing the complexities of the system the autonomic nervous system can control elements of the cardiac cycle.

The parasympathetic nerves in *the Vagus nerve* supply the nodes and the muscles of the atria. Stimulation from these nerves has a tendency to reduce the overall heart rate or force of the beat. The sympathetic nerves have the opposite effect. These influences control the force and rate of the heart to allow for it to adapt to particular circumstances.

Review of the electrical impulses through the heart

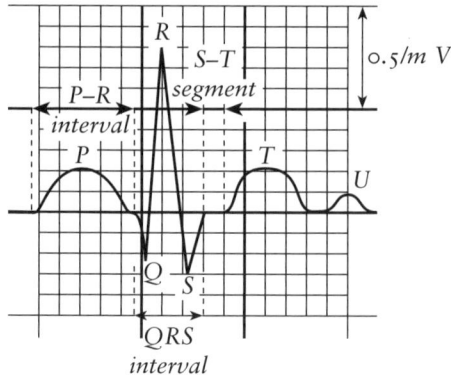

P–R interval adult – 0.18–0.2 sec
child – 0.15–0.18 sec

QRS interval   – 0.07–0.1 sec

Normal ranges of intervals on the ECG

This is commonly done by the ECG (electrocardiogram). In a normal cycle the heart will have some five waves of activity, labelled P–T. Each wave or letter indicates a part of the heart which has been subject to electrical stimulation. The P wave demonstrates that there is an impulse of the contraction over the atria (both right and left). The QRS waves represent the spreading of the contraction through from the AV node to the purkinje fibres, i.e. throughout the ventricular area. The T wave is the relaxation of the ventricular muscle after the contraction. This will be followed by the P wave again as a wave of contraction flows through the atria.

Records – signs of cardiac disease and conditions

The records relating to a patient would normally be as follows:–

1. GP referral letter
2. Ambulance records
3. Clerking notes
4. Inpatient and admission notes
5. outpatient clinic records
6. results and reports
7. operative records
8. Nursing records
9. Chart

It is the Clerking records which would usually contain a review of:

1. Current complaint
2. Past medical history
3. Social History
4. Family history
5. History of current complaint
6. On examination
7. For tests and investigations
8. Possible diagnosis

Out of the "History of current complaint" the symptoms to look for in establishing signs of cardiac disease would be:

- Breathing problems
- Cardiac Pain
- Palpations
- Syncope (fainting)
- Fatigue
- Oedema (excess fluid)
- Arrhythmias – abnormal heart rhythm

Breathing

The types of breathing problems to look for are as follows:

- Dyspnoea: shortness of breath
- SOB: Shortness of breath
- SOBOE: Shortness of breath on exertion
- Orthopnoea: shortness of breath which occurs when lying flat.
- Nocturnal: shortness of breath that occurs at night – called paroxysmal nocturnal dyspnaea (PND)
- Cheynes Stokes respiration: Alternative breathing patterns. Characteristic of morphine administration and terminal illness. Long pauses between breaths
- Apnoea: Absence of breathing.

Cardiac Pain

The types of pain to be aware of are

Angina pectoris (Known simply as angina)

Caused by lack of oxygen to the heart muscle (myocardium) and usually due to poor blood supply to the heart. The muscle can recover from the attack if treated effectively.

Myocardial Infarction (heart attack)

This is caused by the above but the deficit in oxygen is such that the muscle can not recover from the deprivation of oxygen and dies.

Some MIs are silent – i.e. they occur without warning pain and without detection at the time. They can be later identified by an abnormal ECG.

Precordial catch

This is a left stabbing pain and is often associated with anxiety and effort.

Other causes of chest pain include:

- problems with valves (prolapsed)
- oesophageal disease

- blood clot in lung
- high blood pressure in the lungs
- pleurisy
- pneumothorax (collapse of lung/s)
- aortic aneurysm (weakness in wall of aorta – main artery taking blood from lungs to body)

Palpitations

This is the awareness of the heart beat. It is associated with anxiety, stress, caffeine excess and many other factors. It can be associated with abnormal heart rhythms.

Syncope

This is another word for fainting. The different types are as follows:

Vasovagal

The pooling of blood in a particular area often due to shock.

Stokes Adams Attack

The disturbance of the cardiac rhythm. It is usually a very slow heart rate due to some form of block to the rhythm.

Other causes

- High blood pressure in lungs (pulmonary hypertension).
- Blood clot in upper section of heart (atrial thrombus).
- Rhythm problems.
- Valve problems (associated with artificial or narrowed valves).

Fatigue

This is shown by tiredness and lethargy. It is usually due to poor levels of oxygen. It is sometimes drug related.

Oedema

This is excessive fluid in tissues (salt and water retention).

It is treated with diuretics (medication to induce passing urine) or dietary control in patients with minor problems. Dietary control usually reduces salt intake.

Examination of the Cardiac Patient

Examination is by looking at the following indicators:–

- Appearance
- Pulse
- Blood pressure
- Sounds
- Palpation

Appearances

- Cyanosis –
  (discolouration of tissue due to lack of oxygen in blood). This can be CENTRAL – tongue/lips discoloured or it can be PERIPHERAL – finger tips /toes – usually associated with a blue tinge.
- Haemorrhages: (tiny breakages in blood vessels) known as SPLINTER haemorrhages
- Clubbing: Nails bend round on selves – appearance of being curved – sign of insufficient oxygen supply over period of time.

JVP (Jugular Venous Pulse)

Examination of the veins in the neck. Abnormal in heart failure and some valve problems.

Pulse

The pulse can be taken:

- Arterially – (usually in wrist)

- Carotid – (in extreme illness can be seen)
- Radial – Also arterial – in wrist)
- Central – Pulse in heart (taken by stethoscope) or apex

Issues to consider further are:

- Regularity
- Irregularity
- Fast (tachycardia)
- Slow (bradycardia)
- Strength
- Weakness (thready)
- Alternating strong/weak (known as pulsus alternans)

Blood pressure

Blood pressure can be:–

- Systolic (upper figure and rate when blood pumped from heart through body)
- Diastolic (lower figure and rate at rest)
  (Increasing age = increasing blood pressure – usually reflected in systolic.)
- Hypertension: high blood pressure
- Hypotension: low blood pressure
  (**See** Charts Section on pulse and blood pressure)

Auscultation

This is examination by listening to the heart.

Heart sounds result from the closure of the valves in the heart. They occasionally relate to the opening of the valves but this would not be considered normal and would require further investigation.

There are four main valves:

- The tricuspid – between the upper and lower chambers of the right side of the heart
- The pulmonary – between the right lower chamber and the blood vessels (the pulmonary artery) to the lungs
- The mitral valve between the upper and lower chambers of the left side of the heart

- The aortic valve between the lower left chamber and the aorta (the main artery into the body).

Heart sounds

Heart sounds are described as S1, S2, and occasionally if present, S3 and S4.

S1 – Coincides with the closure of the mitral and tricuspid valve closure. It usually occurs at the onset of the ventricular systole (contraction of the ventricle).

Most of the sound usually comes from the closure of the mitral valve.

Occasionally a split sound is heard (One valve closes before the other creating two parts to one heart sound rather than the simultaneous sound of the two valves closing together).

S2 – coincides with the closure of the aortic and pulmonary valves. During breathing out (expiration) this can be heard as a single sound. During inspiration (breathing in) an increased amount of blood returning to the right side of the heart can lead to a delay in the closure of the pulmonary valve. This produces a split sound – being the sound of the aortic valve closing followed by the pulmonary valve.

S3 – occasionally occurs early in the diastolic phase (resting phase) and is associated with the opening of the valves between the upper and lower chambers of the heart. It is sometimes present in younger people but tends to disappear after 40 years of age. It can also be present when there is a fever; anaemia; in pregnancy, and in thyroid conditions.

If it is present after the age of 40 – it is often associated with left ventricular failure.

S4 – is usually associated with the contraction of the upper chambers and appears in the resting phase of the heart beat (diastolic). It is usually a problem which requires investigations. It is usually one of the following:–

- Hypertension (raised blood pressure)
- Aortic stenosis
- Cardiomyopathy

Thrill – a palpable vibration caused by a valve problem.

Typical conditions and sounds: (S1/S2)

Condition/ description	Expiration: S1	Expiration: S2	Inspiration: S1	Inspiration: S2
Exaggerated splitting Right bundle branch block	No split	Small split – hear aorta then pulmonary valve	No split	Large split – aorta then pulmonary valve
Reverse split aortic stenosis	Heard on one side – no split	Large split – hear pulmonary then aortic valve	No split	Pulmonary first then aortic valve
Severe aortic stenosis	No split	Only sound of pulmonary valve	No split	Only pulmonary valve sound
Fixed split Atrial septal defect	No split	Aortic then pulmonary valve sound	No split	Aortic then pulmonary valve
Severe pulmonary component – such as Tetralogy of Fallot, congestion	No split	Aortic valve sound only	No split	Aortic valve sound only

Murmurs

These are vibrations caused by the turbulent blood flow through the heart. They produce an uneven rustling sound.

They are categorised by:

a. Loudness
b. Quality
c. Location
d. Timing

Loudness

Occasionally categorised 1–6 as follows:–

1. Faintest detectable
2. faint but readily detectable
3. Moderately loud
4. Loud
5. Very loud
6. extra loud

Quality

This is the type of sound and is very subjective.

Location

Murmurs are heard by listening with a stethoscope to the chest wall. This determines the origins of the murmur. It will tend to radiate in the direction of the blood flow.

Timing

Systolic – while the heart is contracting. This can be mid-systolic (in the middle of the contraction) or pan systolic – through entire systolic period)

Mid systolic is often also known as an EJECTION murmur.

It develops where there is some turbulence in the left and right ventricles where blood flows from them to the aorta or pulmonary artery.

If it is heard over the area of the aorta it is possibly the sign of aortic stenosis or cardiomyopathy.

If heard over the pulmonary artery then it could be a sign of pulmonary stenosis or tetrology of fallot.

Pansystolic is caused usually by regurgitation of incompetent valves, either mitral or tricuspid valve or ventricular septal defect.

Diastolic murmurs

These may be high pitched and evident at the beginning of the resting or diastolic phase. They may be low pitched and occur in the middle of the diastolic phase.

Sometimes they are categorised as early and mid diastolic. They may be due to regurgitation through the aortic valve or narrowing (stenosis) of the mitral valve.

Continuous murmur

This is patent ductus areteriosus (channel connecting pulmonary artery to aorta in fetus. Closes shortly after birth normally).

Palpation

Types are:–

- Feel for APEX beat – if abnormal
  (i.e.: heavier or lesser than normal)
- Thrill – murmur which can be felt.

Investigations

1. ECG: electrocardiogram

The detailed analysis of the ECG is outside the scope of this book but there are some rhythms which arise from time to time which may require further investigation.

As a general rule those rhythms relating to problems in the ventricles are more serious.

Rhythm problems may be treated by:

- Medication (digoxin or amiodarone)
- Pacing – external pacing – box similar to pacemaker placed outside of body but attached by wires to the heart to supplement current of heart
- internal pacing – usually a pacemaker inserted often under local anaesthetic which takes over or supplements the natural heart beat.
- Electro conversion (usually called cardioversion) – use of the defibrillation machine – allows for an amount of electrical

activity to be placed through the heart causing it to shock itself out of the abnormal rhythm and return to some form of normal rate.

- Where there are frequent rhythm problems which requires this form of treatment an internal defibrillation machine is often inserted which will do this automatically once it detects problems with the heart rate or rhythm.
- Surgery – In some cardiac centres it is possible to undergo electrophysiological tests which map out the pathways of electrical current. These can then be ablated (burnt out).

Common rhythms include the following:

Sinus rhythm SR

This is the normal cardiac rhythm. It varies depending on age, activity and level of fitness. The usual adult rate at rest is 70–80 beats per minute and regular.

Bradycardia

This is where the heart rate is slower than 60 beats per minute (adult range).

Tachycardia

This is where the heart rate is above 100 beats per minute (adult range).

Differing types of tachycardia result from particular sections of the heart.

Sinus tachycardia or bradycardia

This is regular but fast or slow heart rate.

Blocks

There are a variety of heart rhythms known as blocks – i.e. where the electrical impulse is delayed or prevented from getting through effectively.

Blocks vary in severity between 1st – 3rd degree (3rd degree = complete block). There are a large number of causes of blocks.

Atrial

The descriptions of rhythm which commence with Atrial mean that the problem arises in the upper section of the heart which pumps blood to the lower part of the heart.

Atrial fibrillation – AF
- chaotic atrial (upper chamber) activity
- heart remains working satisfactorily, possible discomfort

Atrial flutter
- characteristically shows a saw tooth flutter on the ECG – similar significance to Atrial fibrillation

Supra ventricular tachycardia SVT (literally "above the ventricle" tachycardia)
- more serious form of atrial rhythm problem
- Increased beat to 150–200 beats per minute

Ventricular

The descriptions of rhythm which commence with ventricular mean that the problem arises in the lower section of the heart which pumps blood to the lungs (right side) or the rest of the body (left side). Ventricular rhythm problems are usually more serious in nature and effect.

Ventricular tachycardia VT
- serious problem of very rapid beat – defined as three or more consecutive ventricular beats at more than 120 beats per minute. Often 120–200 beats per minute.
- Emergency situation.

Ventricular fibrilliation VF
- completely disorganized arrhythmias characterised by irregular waves and no effective output.
- Emergency situation.

2. Exercise ECG

This test is to review the difference in heart rate and rhythm when at rest and when exercising and can demonstrate whether the patient has angina.

3. Enzyme Tests

These can indicate when a heart attack has occurred – (myocardial infarction).

Enzyme	Normal Adult Range	Peak time	Issues
Creatinine Kinase (CK)	Man–25–195IU/I Woman 25–170 IU/I	24 hours	Also produced when damage to brain
Aspartate Aminotransferase AST	8–40 IU/I	24–48 falls after 72 hours	Also released when damage to kidney, liver and lungs
Lactate dehydrogenase LDH	120–280 IU/I	3–4 days elevation remains for 10–14 days	Also released when damaged liver and red blood cells
Troponins	Varies	Rise after 6 hours	Being used more often to rule out cardiac pain

4. Other Tests

Echocardiography

This uses an ultrasound probe to examine the valves of the heart and the function of the heart muscle.

Doppler

This evaluates the direction and velocity of blood flow.

Cardiac catheter

This is where radio opaque dye is inserted via the femoral or brachial arteries (groin/arm) that travels back to the heart and the action of the heart can be viewed. Demonstrates the condition of the coronary arteries, which supply the heart muscle itself.

Common Conditions

The following represent the most common cardiac conditions:

1. Ischaemic Heart Disease

This results from either a deficiency in supply of oxygen, or, inadequate supply relative to needs of myocardium.
   It can be caused by:

Most common causes:
- blood clots causing blockages (thrombosis)
- build up of fatty substances causing blockages (atheroma)
- rigidity in the blood vessel (atherosis)
- anaemia
- low blood pressure

or from vastly increased demands such as
- exercise
- thyrotoxicosis

Ischaemic heart disease essentially is a condition which causes a deficiency in oxygen to the heart muscles. It is usually divided into

a. angina pectoris (stable – identified by chest pain when exercising; unstable – chest pain at rest)

b. myocardial infarction – heart attack leading to permanent damage.

2. Myocardial Infarction (MI)

This is the medical term for heart attack. They can occur silently. When diagnosed they need treatment as an emergency.

Summary of the Angina, MI and Rheumatic Fever Records

Condition	Signs	Investigations	Treatment and issues
Angina – can be stable or unstable	Dyspnoea (shortness of breath), pain, fatigue and syncope (fainting)	ECG Exercise ECG Angiography (cardiac catheter)	Acute attack – GTN medication and Beta Blockers Long term medication – aspirin Angioplasty CABG
Myocardial Infarction (MI) heart attack	All cardiac symptoms but some may be silent as can heart attack	ECG enzymes blood pressure and pulse	Acute – medication fibrinolytic medication and pain relief. Oxygen. Post MI – surgery may be indicated (CABG)
Rheumatic fever	Cardiac failure fever and joint pain loss appetite	ECG murmur temperatures throat swab for Strephtococcus Blood test for M C & S ESR (rate should be raised)	Antibiotics High dose of salicylates (aspirin) Steroids

3. Valve disease and problems

The heart has a number of valves which prevent the blood flowing back through particular sections of the heart. The main valves are the mitral, the tricuspid, the pulmonary and the aortic.

Review of Clinical Records

Valve problem	Signs	Investigations	Treatment
Mitral valve stenosis (Restriction of the valve between the left atrium and ventricles – upper and lower chambers) MVS	Usually not apparent until quite stenosed. Cough – blood and frothy weakness fatigue palpitations cyanosis – blueness due to lack of oxygen irregular pulse	Chest x-ray – see small heart with enlarged left atrium (top chamber) ECG can show atrial fibrillation cardiac catheter only if echo does not provide definitive view	Mild – may not need treatment more stenosed – surgery valve replacement usually rheumatic cause
Mitral regurgitation Flow of blood goes back into left atrium M Regurg	Dyspnoea (shortness of breath) Orthopnoea (problems breathing when lying down) fatigue	Heart sounds are soft but prominent third heart sound thrill pansystolic murmur chest x-ray shows left atrial and ventricular enlargement (large left side of heart) ECG – features of atrial fibrillation echo shows dilated left atrium and ventricle catheter only if necessary	Moderate – diuretics may assist major – may need replacement surgery
Aortic stenosis – blockage or restriction in the main valve between the heart and the rest of the body AS	Usually asymptomatic until severe syncope death if no treatment	Abnormal pulse soft heart sounds palpitations ECG abnormal ventricles chest x-ray nothing unusual normally. Echo – thickened cusps on valve catheter recommended	Rest surgery recommended replacement

Valve problem	Signs	Investigations	Treatment
Aortic regurgitation – some of the blood flows back into the left ventricle (lower section of heart)	Bounding pulse	Chest x-ray – Left ventricle enlarged ECG – sinus rhythm echo – dilated Left ventricle cardiac catheter – outline and very irregular	Prophylactic antibiotics and surgery
Tricuspid Stenosis Blockage or restriction between the upper (atrial) and lower (ventricle) section of the right side of heart TS	Murmur (mid systolic)	Chest x-ray – prominent right bulge ECG enlarged R atrium echo – thickened valve Cardiac catheter – shows enlargement of atrium	Surgery
Tricuspid regurgitation causes blood to flow back into the upper right side of heart (Right Atrium)	Palpable liver Atrial fibrillation. Pan systolic murmur	ECG Chest x-ray	Surgery (occasionally required)
Pulmonary Stenosis – restriction of blood flow through the valve from the right ventricle/lower chamber and the blood vessel leading to the lungs PS	Fatigue Syncope (fainting) Murmur – ejection systole 4th heart sound	Heart sounds 4th present. Delayed soft component of S2. Chest x-ray – prominent pulmonary artery ECG cardiac catheter – shows level and degree of stenosis	Balloon valvotomy (insertion of tube which can be inflated to force constricting material to the edge of the valve allowing for some access through).
Pulmonary regurgitation (blood flows back into the right lower chamber)	Asymptomatic Early diastolic murmur Second Heart sound	ECG Chest x-ray enlarged heart Echo – dilated ventricle	No treatment often

4. Cardiomyopathies

These are severe chronic heart disorders and include the following

- Dilated – dilatation of the ventricles
- Hypertrophic – thickening of the walls of the ventricles
- Restricted – gradual obliteration of the ventricles

In general many suffer a poor prognosis, although some patients are fortunate to have only minor symptoms.

5. Hypertension

This is abnormal elevation of blood pressure (**see** Blood Pressure in Charts Section as to normal rates).

It is associated with age, sex (male more then female) and pregnancy.

It can lead to heart and kidney problems (both can fail). It can also lead to the development of peripheral vascular disease. It can also be detected by examining the blood vessels at the back of the eye.

Investigations

- Blood pressure usually taken on three separate occasions
- Chest x-ray (may show left ventricular enlargement)
- Urine tests – blood and protein (checking on state of kidneys)
- Blood tests – creatinine and urea (checking on state of kidneys)
- Blood levels of potassium – may need to start diuretic treatment

Treatment

- Diuretics
- Beta blockers
- Calcium antagonists
- ACE inhibitors

6. Heart failure

This is a cardiac disorder which prevents the delivery of sufficient oxygen to meet the requirements of the rest of the body. It can be left or right sided, acute or chronic. Left sided is a more serious condition.
Where it is minor it is likely to be asymptomatic.

Review of Clinical Records

Condition of Acute RIGHT sided heart failure	Condition of Acute LEFT sided heart failure
Reduction in cardiac output (amount of blood pushed through system) Cool skin and reduction in blood pressure Peripheral cyanosis (toes and fingers blue colour) fatigue Liver congestion Loss of appetite Oedema	Abrupt shortness of breath and orthopnoea – i.e. worse when lying flat Pink, frothy fluid in lungs Central cyanosis – blue lips reduced blood pressure Reduction and cessation in production of urine (oliguria) Low cardiac output – reduction in volume of blood flowing through heart increase in heart rate (tachycardia) coolness peripheral cyanosis – blueness in fingers and toes

The problems which occur with all heart failures are:

- arrhythmias are common
- development of deep vein thrombosis is common
- development of pulmonary emboli – clots in lungs causing obstruction
- major organs begin to fail
- increasing problems as heart failure continues

ACUTE HEART FAILURE = EMERGENCY

7. Infections

Infections will be:–

- Myocarditis – infection of the myometrium or muscle layer of the heart – usually caused by a virus, may cause heart failure

- Endocarditis – infection of the inner layer of the heart. Occasionally results from dental procedures
- Pericarditis – infection of the outer layer

All infections are potentially very serious and needs to be treated urgently.

The examination will include:–

- Full blood count (FBC)
- Biochemistry review and blood taken for culture and sensitivity (U + E. Blood for C + S)
- Echocardiography (Echo)
- Chest x-ray (CXR)
- Erythrocyte sedimentation rate will be increased (ESR)
- Electrocardiogram (ECG)
- Blood pressure, pulse and temperature (BP, P, T → "obs")

The treatment may include the use of antibiotics and or surgery. It will depend on the bacterial cause as to which antibiotic is chosen. Penicillin and gentamycin are the most common.

The patient may require surgery if the condition deteriorates. The infection can cause damage to valves and cause emboli (clots and blockages) to form. Heart failure can also occur.

8. Congenital Heart Disease

Review and summary

Defect	Problem	Signs	Investigation	Treatment
Ventricular septal defect V SD	Hole between the ventricles leading to deoxygenated blood mixing with oxygenated blood in the ventricles	Loud and long systolic murmur Fatigue Dyspnoea (difficulty in breathing) Cardiac enlargement Increasing blood pressure	Large defects on x-ray Large defects ECG – left and right ventricular signs Echocardiography Doppler	Surgery in large or symptomatic cases

Defect	Problem	Signs	Investigation	Treatment
Atrial septal defect A SD	Hole between atria as above	Often asymptomatic in children Dyspnoea Fatigue Weakness Heart sounds altered (Loud) Murmur – mid systolic ejection	Chest x-ray – prominent pulmonary artery ECG – right bundle branch block Echo – hypertrophy (enlargement) Doppler – flow disturbance Catheter often not necessary	Large – surgery
Persistent Ductus Arteriosus PDA	Failure of ductus arteriosus to close after birth (DA is passage between pulmonary arteries and aorta (mixing deoxygenated and oxygenated blood). Closes normally at birth, open while in uterus	Murmur Thrill often felt Peripheral pulse bounding	X-ray can see aorta and pulmonary system ECG abnormal Echocardiogram shows dilated left atrium and left ventricle	Premature infants – indomethicin treatment Other cases – surgery as soon as possible
Coarctation of aorta	Narrowing of the aorta	High blood pressure in upper section of body Often asymptomatic Delayed pulse in lower limbs Murmur	Chest x-ray – indentation at site of coarctaton and notching of ribs. ECG – left ventricular hypertrophy Echocardiography – sometimes shows problem MRI scan	Surgery – excise section

Defect	Problem	Signs	Investigation	Treatment
Fallots tetralogy	4 problems – restriction (stenosis) of pulmonary artery VSD – ventricular septal defect Aortic misplacement Right ventricular hypertrophy	Children Dyspnoea Fatigue Cyanosis (turning blue) Systolic ejection murmur Finger clubbing	Chest x-ray – large right ventricle ECG – right ventricular hypertrophy Echocardiogram – discontinuity between aorta and anterior wall Angiography needed for scale and degree of problem	Surgery

Example of the Records of A Cardiac Patient

H/O Complaint	History of current complaint:
Central chest pain	Central chest pain
Radiating L arm	Radiating down left arm
SOB	Shortness of breath
1 episode 1/52 ago	One previous episode one week ago
10 mins	Lasted 10 minutes
PMHx	Previous medical history:
COAD	Chronic asthma/bronchitis
Angina∆ 3yrs ago	Angina diagnosed three years ago
Nil Else	Nil else of significance

FHx	Family history:
Father RIP MI 55 yrs	Father died at 55 following heart attack
Mother CVA 67 yrs	Mother had stroke 67 years of age
2 kids 21/17 divorced	Two children – 21 and 17 Divorced
SHx	Social history:
Smokes 20/day. Alcohol in moderation	Smokes 20 per day. Drinks in moderation
Obese - tv repairman	Overweight. Works as tv repairman
O/E	On examination
SOB at rest	Shortness of breath even at rest
Tachycardic, Irreg	Rapid but irregular heart rate
Hypotensive	Low blood pressure
Central cyanosis	Blue lips
Anxious, sweaty	Anxious Sweaty
HS ° murmurs	Heart sounds No murmurs
Δ? MI, ??? Angina	Diagnosis: Possible heart attack Alternative possible diagnosis of angina
For: ECG	For Electrocardiogram
Enzymes	Bloods taken for cardiac enzyme testing
FBC	Also for full blood count

Obs 15/mins	Pulse, respirations and blood pressure every 15 minutes
2L O2 GTN SL	24% Oxygen provided Glycerol tri-nitrate given under tongue
Refer - cardiology	For referral to cardiology team
Results - enzymes +	Results: enzymes positive
ECG - MI	Electrocardiogram shows heart attack
Admit CCU. Monitor	To admit to coronary care unit Monitor to be kept in place
Continuous O2 Streptokinase IV	Continuous oxygen Streptokinase infusion intravenously
NOK informed. Transfer CCU	Relatives informed transfer to Coronary Care Unit

Paediatrics

Paediatrics

Neonatal Review and Development

Definition

A neonate is an infant less than 28 days of age

	Apgar Scores		
	0 score	**1 score**	**2 scores**
Heart rate	Absent	<100 beats per minute	>100 beats per minute
Respiratory effort	Absent	Gasping, irregular	Regular and strong
Muscle tone	Flaccid	Some flexion of limbs	Well flexed and active
Reflex irritability	None	Grimace	Cry or cough
Colour	Pale or blue	Body pink but extremities blue	Pink

Examination of the newborn

1. Apgar scores (see above) Taken at birth, one minute and five minutes to demonstrate condition of neonate at birth.

2. Head circumference and other measurements to ensure consistent on centile (all body measurements consistent with each other).

   All children are measured via a graph that plots between 10 and 90% children's growth. The size, length or weights are plotted against gestational age. Those children who fall below the 10th centile line are considered small for their gestational age.

Those who appear above the 90th centile are considered large for gestational age.

Not all babies who fall below the 10th centile are pre term (less than 37 weeks of pregnancy completed) although this is more common.

3. Fontanelle (soft space in skull of infant before skull bones close by 2 years) – size varies considerably but should not be tense. A tense fontanelle is possibly a sign of increased pressure in brain. Ultrasound needed.

4. Breathing and chest wall.

5. Heart – to check pulse is satisfactory. Normal rate for newborn baby – 110–150 beats per minute when awake. Premature babies have increased heart rate. Also femoral pulses (on leg) to check no cardiac problems

6. Abdominal examination – no masses. Check liver.

7. Genitalia and anus

8. Colour – E.g. pale may mean anaemia.

9. Jaundice – common in pre term babies requiring photo therapy (affects approximately 50% children in some form)

10. Palate and mouth – check for cleft palate

11. Hips – E.g., congenital dislocation of hip

12 Eyes – check for cataracts

13. Back and spine – check for straightness and for spina bifida

14. Muscle tone – check not flaccid (lacks rigidity, soft)

Term

- Term babies: Between 38–42 weeks
- Post term: More than 42 weeks
- Pre term: less than 37 weeks

Development of the child

	6–8 weeks	6–9 months	18–24 months	3–4 years
Examination	Growth charts & centiles Eyes – exclude cataracts Congenital dislocation of hip checked	Growth charts & centiles Testicles – descended in boys Congenital dislocation of hip checked	Growth charts & centiles Check for squints Check for anaemia	Growth charts & centiles Testicular descent in boys
Language/ Hearing	Normal cry and responds to noise	Turns towards sound. Distraction test	No problems noted by parents	Can provide name Enough speech for stranger to understand
Gross motor skills	Four limbs move symmetrically Normal muscle tone	Sits without support Pulls to standing	Walks well Kicks ball	Can hop
Fine motor skills	Eyes follow object	Reaches for objects Palmar grasp Can pass from one hand to other	Scribbles Tower of blocks – 6 × 3 cms high	Can draw circle or cross Builds bridge when shown from cubes
Social skills	Smiles	Solid food in mouth	Removes garments Feeds self with spoon	Names other people Washes hands Eats with knife and fork Make believe play Hears and tell stories
Special Senses		Distraction hearing test Check for squint	Check for squint	Hearing test if necessary Ophthalmic test if necessary

Clerking or review notes

These are the same as with all areas:

- Current complaint – what complaining of   C/O
- Past Medical History   PMHx
- Family History   FHx
- Social History   SHx
- History of presenting complaint   HPC
- On examination   O/E
- Possible diagnosis or impression   Imp/
- Investigations to be completed.   For:

History

The most important factor in the taking of a history or examination of the child is the child's age.

Areas to consider:

- *Systemic* – has there been any change to bowel habits, eating, breathing, degree of activity and personality
- *Past medical history* of note – N.B. with small child, mother's obstetric history may be relevant
- *Family history* – particularly if considering a congenital abnormality
- *Social History* – school or sibling problems
- *Development* – check milestones and whether at appropriate level

Examination

Cardiac System

- Pulse
- Auscultation (heart sounds)
- Murmur
- Palpation
- Liver

Pulse

Pulse rates vary at different ages

More than 12 years	normal adult pulse 60–100
5–12	80–120
2–5	90–140
Less than 1 year	110–160

All rates will be increased where there is a sign of infection, anxiety or exercise.

Heart Sounds

Listening to the heart sound can demonstrate in a healthy child some sounds which are the result of the valves closing.
(**See** Cardiac Section.)

Murmurs

Many children have murmurs that disappear over time and are not found at adult hood.

Murmurs are often graded according to their loudness and timing. It is also possible to detect a vibration with some murmurs when palpating (examination by touch) the chest. This is known as a thrill.

Murmurs occur as a result of congenital heart problems (**see** cardiac system).

Signs

Murmur requires further investigation or review to see if there is:

- Loudness
- Pan systolic
- Diastolic
- Thrill
- Other cardiac signs and symptoms

Palpation

This is the examination by feeling the area.

In cardiac review a murmur, which can be felt because of vibration, is a THRILL.

Other signs to look out for are if it is possible to palpate a tap in the right ventricle then this is possibly a sign of failure of the right ventricle.

Liver problems

In small children liver failure can indicate problems with the heart. Palpating (feeling) the liver can demonstrate whether the liver is enlarged (HEPATOMEGALY).

Respiratory System

- Breathing
- Palpation
- Auscultation – breath sounds

Breathing

Signs to be looked for are:

- Grunting or noisy expiration
- Use of other muscles (the accessory muscles – chest wall rises significantly)
- Difficulty feeding or sleeping
- Increased respiratory rate

Respiratory rates in children:

Teenage +	15–20 per minute
Young children (up to 12)	20–30
Infants (up to 5)	20–40
Neonates	30–50

An increase in rate is likely when exercise has been completed, the child is anxious or an infection is present. Increased rate is called TACHYPNOEA.

Palpation

In children of school age chest expansion can be checked. It should be between 3–5 c.m.s.

Auscultation

Signs to be looked out for are:

- Crackles – problems with the bronchioles usually caused by infection in the lung
- Wheeze – high pitched on expiration – obstruction usually caused by mucus
- Stridor – harsh low-pitched sound on inspiration – obstruction at top end of respiratory tract
- Hoarseness – problem with vocal cords

Examination of the abdomen

- Inspection
- Palpation
- Auscultation

Inspection

Check whether abdomen is distended and/or tender.

Palpation

Check for problems with spleen, liver or kidney.

Right upper quadrant of abdomen if intussusception possible (Where one section of intestine in infant becomes lodged in another section causing obstruction)

Auscultation

Check to see if sounds from bowel are satisfactory.

Investigations

Most forms of investigation are available in paediatrics as elsewhere. There are some tests, which are more commonly undertaken in paediatrics however:

- LP Lumbar puncture – removal of cerebro spinal fluid to test for infection (possible meningitis)
- Sweat test – test for cystic fibrosis – depends on the level of sodium (Na) and chlorine (Cl) in sweat
- Barium (Ba) meal – for problems with gastric system
- Oscillometric tests – tests for blood pressure in very young infants

When considering any test for paediatrics always check whether the values are likely to be the same as for an adult. The range of acceptable levels is often very different.

Haematology

Haemoglobin initially reduces after birth from very high levels (14–21.5 g/dl) to 9.0–13 g/dl within first two to three months. Thereafter it increases:

1 year	11–14 g/dl
5 years	11.5–13.5 g/dl
10 years	11.5–15.5 g/dl
15 years	13–16 g/dl (male)
	12–16 g/dl (female)

White cell count will also decrease:

Birth	10–26 × 10 9/l
1 year	6–18 × 10 9/l
5 years	5–17 × 10 9/l
10 years	4–5–15 × 10 9/l
15 years	4.5–13 × 10 9/l

Biochemistry

Common tests and ranges

Substance	Approximate Age/Stage	Average Range
Albumin	Neonate Child	25–36 g/l 35–55 g/l
Blood gases Arterial	pO2 PCO2	11–14 kPa 4.5–6 kPa
Creatinine	1–11 years	20–80 mol
Glucose	2 years	3–6 mmol
Potassium	Infant Child	3.5–6 mmol 3.3–4.9 mmol
Sodium	Child	133–145 mmol

Medical Records: General Principles

The general principles to follow when considering medical records are:–

1. Medications

Whenever medications are provided check the weight of the child. Nurses are specially educated (even when training) to deal with paediatric dosages, which can often be very confusing.

If in doubt check paediatric dose in BNF (British National Formulary) or other formulary to ensure that it is correct.

2. Review

As children deteriorate or change condition much quicker than adults it is necessary to check for frequent reviews by nurses or medical staff.

3. Symptoms

Children are not always accurate historians and do not always demonstrate symptoms which are easily identifiable. E.g.: they can complain of hunger when in pain, therefore it is important to check objective tests and investigations such as charts, results and reports.

Masking

Children's symptoms can also be masked effectively, e.g., children may be distracted, or, children may receive pain relief more easily because of the distress pain causes and their lack of understanding. They may mask complaints of pain.

Parents

Parents often know children best and can interpret symptoms. A good paediatric nurse or paediatrician will recognize the value in parents' analysis of the child's condition or symptoms.

Common problems in neonates

Checklist for medical records

Condition	Signs	Investigations	Issues
Respiratory Distress (Problems with breathing)	Rapid breathing (Tachypnoea) Noisy on expiration Blue colour (cyanosis) Laboured breathing	Chest x-ray Blood gases Check for respiratory rate Heart sounds and rates Bloods for haemoglobin and check acidosis	In pre term infants teated with surfactant – substance which lowers tension between surfaces in lungs. Large possible number of causes

Condition	Signs	Investigations	Issues
Obstruction	Vomiting – bile, (yellow in appearance) Distension of abdomen	X-ray of abdomen Other tests – to ensure electrolyte balance ok – full blood count and biochemistry	May require emergency surgery
Jaundice	Yellowish or dusky appearance	Blood for haemoglobin, White cell count and reticulocyte count Blood bilirubin level checked Blood film Check for Rhesus incompatibility Direct Coombes test Urine specimen Thyroid function tests	Many different causes – accurate history as to when it developed v important. If serum bilirubin >85 umol/litre clinically significant Prolonged jaundice is particularly significant and may require Liver scan, Ultra sound, clotting studies and mini laparatomy
Infection	Increased temperature Increased irritability Vomiting Lethargy Poor feeding and weight gain Breathing difficulties Distended abdomen or bulging/tense fontanelle Shock/cardiac problems	Full blood count Temperature pulse. Blood pressure and respiratory rate Microbiology specimens – urine, stool X-ray or scan Lumbar puncture	Numerous causes. Bulging or tight fontanelle – emergency possible meningitis

Emergency Conditions

All conditions in children are likely to warrant more rapid and urgent attention than the equivalent in adults because children are less able to cope with illness or trauma. On the whole children are able to suffer from the same conditions or accidents as adults but some emergencies are perhaps more common than others.

a. Laryngeal obstruction

This occurs where the throat is blocked (and more importantly the windpipe or TRACHEA) due to a number of causes including:

- EPIGLOTTITIS (inflammation of the epiglottis) or
- CROUP (inflammation of the throat structures due to a virus) or even
- A foreign body stuck in the throat (such as a small toy).

If there is a complete obstruction and the child can barely breathe a paediatric anaesthetist is required who will:

a. Intubate (Place a slim tube down the back of the throat or via the nose to maintain a pathway for oxygen into the lungs) The tube is known as an ETT (endo tracheal tube)

b. Provide extra oxygen

If this proves impossible because the throat is closed or blocked completely a tracheotomy is required, where a tube is eventually inserted into the neck below the level of the blockage.

Unless there is no one qualified available the procedure should only be undertaken by highly experienced medical staff.

Problems

a. Lack of oxygen to the heart will cause death of some tissues and may stop the heart completely (MYOCARDIAL INFARCTION)

b. Lack of oxygen to the brain may lead to some brain damage

c. The throat is very vascular and contains a number of important structures. It is easy in an inexperienced practitioner to cause extensive bleeding.

d. Time is of the essence.

b. Febrile Children

Febrile children are children with a high temperature.

Most high temperatures are caused by viral or bacterial infection for which rest, fluids and medications to reduce the temperature or treat the infection are sufficient. Some however, are caused by more serious infections, which have potentially fatal consequences.

The following should be reviewed when presented with a child with a high temperature:

- Past medical history
- Family illnesses – particularly recent
- Immunisation status
- Travel abroad
- Contact with animals
- Any predisposition to infection due to HIV problems, problems with immune system such as in Leukaemia.

Examination and review

The following areas need particularly close examination:–

a. **Respiratory system**

N.B. A child can often have a respiratory tract infection and another illness. Some conditions such as pneumonia are difficult to detect without x-ray examination.

b. **Ears**

These should always be examined because otitis media (infection of the inner ear) is common in young children.

c. **Eyes**

It is important to look for any signs of swelling round the eye.

d. Rash

If there is a rash present it is important to note where it is placed and whether it will blanch when a glass is pressed against it. If it does not blanch it could be meningitis and potentially very serious.

e. Stridor (harsh sound during breathing usually associated with obstruction)

A Stridor could demonstrate possible epiglottis or croup or an infection of the trachea, which has caused the trachea to swell.

f. Tonsils

If signs of redness or oozing on tonsils then this could be tonsillitis. Antibiotics may be required depending on severity of the symptoms and the age of child

g. Abdomen

It is often difficult to examine a child and achieve the same response as with adults. It is difficult to ascertain whether particular sections of the abdomen are painful, particularly in young child who will not be able to inform medical staff of problem.

If signs of abdominal pain are present this could be either:

- Appendicitis, or,
- Kidney infection

h. Bowel habits

Diarrhoea may indicate gastro enteritis. This may be resolved with fluids and little or no food. Some infections require antibiotic treatment, particularly if there is mucus or blood in the stool.

i. Urinary habits

A sample of urine should be taken where a child has a temperature that is not resolving.

j. Fits

Any child presenting with fits should be seen urgently.

A high temperature in itself can sometimes lead to fits irrespective of the initial cause of the increase in temperature.

Alternatively a high temperature can be a sign of:

- Serious infection

- Encephalitis/Meningitis (infection in the brain)
- Septicaemia – infection of the blood

k. General energy and well being

A lethargic child may be demonstrating signs of meningitis.

l. Orthopaedic issues

Painful bones or joints suggest a possibility of infection in the area OSTEOMYELITIS.

Neck stiffness can indicate meningitis.

Arching of the back can also indicate meningitis.

Tests

Where an infection is indicated the following tests are usually completed:

- Full blood count – including white cell count
- Urine testing
- Chest x-ray
- Lumbar Puncture to review the CSF (cerebro spinal fluid)
- Observations (pulse, respirations and temperature)

In some conditions further testing is required.

c. Poisoning

In most cases of poisoning the accidental ingestion of household products or medications is involved. Where an older child is the patient (for example an adolescent) the possibility of suicidal intent or psychological distress should be considered.

Evaluation

The process for evaluating the situation is as follows:–

a. Where the child is critically ill treatment follows the standards for all urgent matters. The airway must be seen to be clear, breathing in tact and the circulation (or flow of blood around the body) should be satisfactory. If not then appropriate measures should be taken to deal with the immediate problem.

b. If there are respiratory problems then:–

- Neck should be extended
- Intubate if needed
- Oxygen given

c. Circulatory problems may be due to:–

    (i)   Low and falling blood pressure (usually due in these cases to shock or a reduction in the amount of fluids circulating around the body because blood vessels have dilated and collected large amounts of fluid).

        Increase level and amount of fluid and set up an intravenous infusion.

    (ii)   Rhythm problems with the heart.

        These may require medications to regularise and may require monitoring on the ward or in the A & E department.

    (iii) Neurological problems.

        Fitting (seizures) may require anti-convulsant medication

Identification

Poisons need to be identified since they may have appropriate antidotes, or, alternatively there may be various medications which could react with the poison to cause additional and severe problems.

Action to be taken:

a. **Biochemistry** – blood should be sent for urgent testing to the biochemistry department.

    Guys Hospital in London has a specialist and renowned toxicity unit.

b. **Family** – family members may have some idea of poison ingested – particularly where a young child is involved

c. **Microbiology** – urine tests may be taken which assist with diagnosis

d. **Saturation tests** – level of oxygen in the blood may suggest particular poisons

e. **Blood sugar tests** – some blood tests can be taken on the ward or in the A & E department – for example the level of sugar in the blood.

f. **Appearance of skin** – yellow skin (jaundiced appearance) may suggest paracetamol or iron tablets for example

g. **Odour of breath**

h. **Temperature** – low temperature may suggest carbon monoxide – High temperature may suggest aspirin

i. **Blood pressure measurements:–**
Low blood pressure (HYPOTENSION) suggests possible iron or opiates
High blood pressure (HYPERTENSION) suggests amphetamines.

j. **Heart Rhythms:–**
   - Abnormal rhythm – possibly digoxin (cardiac medication)
   - Slow heart beat (BRADYCARDIA) possibly beta blockers (type of cardiac medication)
   - Fast heart beat (TACHYCARDIA) possibly cocaine or amphetamines

k. **Problems with consciousness:–**
   - Coma – antidepressants, narcotics and sleeping tablets (sedatives)
   - Fits – lead, aspirin and some anti depressants
   - Hallucinations – amphetamines, other controlled or illegal drugs, some anti depressants
   - Delirious – LSD cocaine and heavy metals

l. **Inspection of the eye:–**
   - Small pupil (MEIOSIS) organophosphates, some narcotics
   - Enlarged pupil (MYDRIASIS) some anti depressants

m. **Muscle problems**
   - Weakness or paralysis – heavy metals or organophosphates
   - Increased tonicity (HYPERTONICITY) increased muscle tone – anti emetics (drugs which prevent vomiting or nausea)

n. **Breathing problems**
   * Reduced respiration (HYPOVENTILATION) narcotics and sedatives
   * Increased respiration (HYPERVENTILATION) aspirin

o. **Gastro-intestinal problems** – Often caused by iron, organophosphate ingestion

Treatment

The treatment for poisoning is as follows:–

a. Encourage vomiting (EMESIS)
   Child must be alert
   Child must have gag reflex that is functioning properly

   Do not use where:–

   1. Little or no consciousness
   2. Caustic substances ingested
   3. Petroleum distillate substances ingested
   4. More than 4–5 hours of ingestion unless gastric emptying is delayed because of nature of substance – such as some anti depressants and aspirin.

b. Wash out stomach (GASTRIC LAVAGE)

c. Use activated charcoal – blocks the absorption of some of the poison while in the stomach.

d. Encourage removal of poison from body by assisting with increased urine production (diuresis) or providing a blood transfusion (less common activity.)

e. Antidotes where indicated

f. Extra oxygen provision

g. Extra fluid provision

Poison, Signs and Treatment Chart

Substance	Signs	Tests	Treatment	Issues
Alcohol	Intoxication Drowsiness Smell on breath	Blood sugar Will be affected	Monitor and provide IV glucose if necessary	
Bleach and caustic substances	Local burning, lesions around mouth Vomiting Respiratory distress		Small amounts of milk or water No vomiting or lavage	Endoscopy may be required to check damage Use of steroids to reduce inflammation controversial
Carbon monoxide	Headache shortness of breath, diarrhoea, disorientation and coma Reduced temperature Occasional red flush to skin (rarer)	Blood – chocolate brown colour Blood for carbon monoxide levels Temperature	Where has been or is unconscious, has neurological symptoms (other than headache or nausea) or where level of carbon monoxide in blood is more than 40% hyperbaric – oxygen required. Otherwise Oxygen @ 100% if possible	Restricted facilities for hyper baric treatment
Digoxin	Gastro intestinal disturbances Slow heart rate, Abnormal heart rhythms	ECG tests Blood tests – may have high level of potassium in blood	Gastric lavage/emesis Use activated charcoal Reduce potassium in blood (if raised) Treat abnormal rhythms – pace	Specific antidote for life threatening condition To be used with great care in children. Check dosage carefully

Substance	Signs	Tests	Treatment	Issues
			(control heart beat), medications such as phenytoin, lignocaine	
Disc batteries	Mild gastro-intestinal symptoms Contraction of gullet (oesophagus) with larger batteries	X-rays Check faeces if in for some time	If in stomach for 36–48 hours – remove surgically If develop abdominal symptoms (such as pain or tenderness) remove only if no symptoms wait until passes naturally – rarer	Most foreign bodies do not need removal if passed through oesophagus Probably remove if more than 48 hours in body
Iron	Initially nausea, vomiting and diarrhoea. Followed by Blood in vomit and stools (haematemesis and malaena) Shock and increasing acidity of the body, reduction in consciousness levels Deterioration in liver with increasing times for clotting of blood, jaundice, renal failure and falling blood sugars	Full blood count, including levels of iron Blood glucose levels Electrolytes Plain abdominal x-ray Blood for clotting time	Emesis or gastric lavage Desferri-oxamine 40mg per kg weight (max 1gm) Severe cases IV otherwise intramuscular Correct abnormal levels in blood (More glucose, blood transfusion if necessary)	Serious emergency may require gastrotomy to remove tablets from stomach

Substance	Signs	Tests	Treatment	Issues
Organo-phosphates	Mild – fatigue, headaches, nausea, diarrhoea and abdominal cramps. Severe – confusion, seizures, reduction in respiration, coma and death Other symptoms: Reduced heart beat, blood pressure. Dilated pupils, increased salivation and sweating. Incontinence Smells of garlic	Blood – serum pseudo-cholinesterase Red cell cholinesterase	Decontaminate by washing Emesis/gastric lavage Medications: Atropine Pralidoxime	Start drugs while waiting for results of blood tests if possible Do not use parasympatho-mimetic drugs, Phenothiazines or Antihistamines Where carbamate insecticides involved DO NOT use Pralidoxime
Paracetamol	Gastric irritation After 36 hours – liver and renal failure starts Jaundice, bleeding Encephalo-pathy Low blood pressure Death	Blood levels of paracetamol Clotting times Plasma creatinine and urine volume Blood glucose levels	Emesis/gastric lavage Antidote Oral – methionine (mild) IV acetylcysteine Monitor levels indicated in tests	If more than 15 hours elapsed – antidote probably ineffective Often transferred to specialist unit
Petroleum derivatives	Respiratory difficulties		Prophylactic antibiotics and steroids Additional oxygen if needed	Do not use emesis

Substance	Signs	Tests	Treatment	Issues
Potassium	Diarrhoea, sweating and abdominal cramps ECG changes	ECG tests Blood test – levels of potassium	IV glucose given Diuretics Salbutamol	Consider cause – rare overdose? Renal failure or substantial injuries to tissues
Salicylates (EG Aspirin)	Nausea, vomiting, tinnitus, deafness, fever, reduced blood glucose levels, dehydration, shock, reduction in conscious state, fits and death	Plasma levels salicylates Haematology including clotting times Blood sugars Biochemistry – urea and electrolytes Calcium, liver function tests and arterial gases	Emesis/gastric lavage Charcoal Monitor fluid and electrolyte balance Vitamin K Dialysis if required Correct acidosis by Sodium Hydroxide	Number of biochemical problems including reduced glucose, calcium and potassium Lethal dose in child can be less than 4g and much less in infant
Tricyclic antidepressants	Rapid heart beat, urinary retention, drowsiness, hallucinations, fits, coma, low blood pressure, low temperature (hypothermia), insufficient oxygen (hypoxia) and low potassium in blood, metabolic acidosis, reduction in respirations	ECG – if the QRS segment is more than 100 m/sec possible toxicity Biochemistry tests – blood potassium Observations (temperature pulse and blood pressure)	Gastric lavage Activated charcoal Monitor ECG Sedation if necessary Fluid replacement to increase blood pressure Ventilate if low oxygen levels IV potassium Use bicarbonate if cardiac rhythm problems	Variety of tricyclics available. Most end with triptyline but others are Dothiepin and imipramine. Both very common. No particular relation between level of the drug in the blood system and its effect but 35mg/kg weight could be fatal

Common Medical Problems

Condition	Signs	Examination	Investigation	Issues
Failure to thrive	Sub optimal weight gain or growth	Weight, height, head circumference Hands – clubbing. Anaemia Abdominal distension Murmurs	Test feed Full blood count Urea Creatinine Bicarbonate Urine – send for Microbiology – pH test Electrolytes B12 check Clotting profile Liver function tests Stool testing Sweat test	Linked on occasions to child abuse Need to check for chronic infection, organ failure
Abdominal Pain a. appendicitis	localized tenderness which is worse on moving with increasing severity and low grade temperature	Temperature palpation	Rare that blood and laboratory tests of use	Surgery usually required
Abdominal Pain b. intus-susception (section of bowel becomes inserted into another section)	Colicky pain Distended abdomen Vomiting and diarrhoea Red currant jelly type stool	Dehydrated Temperature Pain on palpation	Abdominal x-ray	Surgery Serious condition – shock is a problem
Diarrhoea and vomiting	Increased frequency in defaecation and vomiting	Increasing dehydration Different appearance of vomit may assist diagnosis (see charts)	Appearance of vomit and diarrhoea. Full blood count Stool test Electrolytes checked Ultrasound scan endoscopy in severe cases	Can be number of different problems including infection. However may be PYLORIC stenosis (restriction in part of stomach) which usually requires surgery

Typical records; e.g. febrile child

Via A & E 3/12 ↑ temp 2/7	Admission via Accident and emergency 3 month old baby with increasing temperature for 2 days
PMHx FTND °H$_x$O of note	Past medical history – full term normal delivery. No other history of note
1 brother - 2 yr OK	1 brother who is 2 and ok
HCC - ° feeding today	History of current complaint – no feeding today
Listless o/n snuffly 2/7	Listless overnight and snuffly for 2 days
↑ temp o/n	Increasing temperature overnight
??? fit this p.m.	Possible fit this afternoon
Lasted 1 min - roll eyes	Lasted one minute with eyes rolling
O/e floppy. Hot. 38.5 degrees	On examination – floppy and hot
cyanosis	Blue appearance to lips
PEARL	Pupils equal and reacting to light
Ears ✓ tonsils ✓	Ears and tonsils ok
° rash ° guarding ° neck stiffness	No rash, guarding (test of abdominal problems) or neck stiffness
° photophobia	No aversion to light
Imp URTI	Impression upper respiratory tract infection
For CXR	For chest x-ray

Swabs	Swabs
FBC	Full blood count
MSU	Mid stream urine
Obs 30 mins/T 15 min	Respirations and pulse to be taken every 30 minutes temperature every 15 minutes
LP	Lumbar puncture
Calpol	For a paracetamol medication to reduce temperature
Admit o/n	Admit overnight

Surgery

Surgery

Medical Records

Operative records include

1. Consent forms
2. Anaesthetic records
3. Operation notes
4. Recovery room records
5. Pre operative checklists
6. Postoperative check lists
7. Day Unit Charts (include all of the above in one booklet).

In addition to the above list the treating surgical team will complete some elements of the pre-operative assessment. Their records are likely to be recorded within the clinical records.

In all forms of surgery there are a number of tests and assessments to be made. The medical records relating to surgery will predominantly be concerned with the recording of these issues.

Pre Operative Period: The Records

The pre-operative period records include:–

1. Consent form
2. Pre operative assessment: anaesthetic record
3. Pre operative assessment: surgical team – clinical records
4. Pre operative checklist – nursing records

Pre operative assessment and tests

The following are the checks, which form part of the usual pre-operative assessment by medical and anaesthetic staff. These should be found in the medical records. Where problems have developed during or in the postoperative period then it is necessary to review the pre-operative checks. These may indicate that the patient did not receive a full or complete assessment, or there were factors, which would have affected postoperative recovery in any event.

1. *History*

Full history is essential – including past medical history and operation, allergies and any complications with previous surgery.

2. *Diagnosis*

Check diagnosis is correct.

3. *Assessment – from history*

Particular note should be considered of the following factors when assessing a patient for surgery. These issues may be detailed in the pre operative assessment of either the anaesthetist or the surgeon. The reasons for their relevance are detailed below:

Assessment Chart

Characteristic	Problem	Issues
Age	Old age does not prevent surgery but increases the risks associated with it.	Depends on nature and effect of condition as to whether surgery worthwhile
Nutrition	Obesity carries with it anaesthetic risks, technically more difficult surgery, increased post operative risks and delay in recovery	Explanation to patient required as to increased risks. May require weight loss pre surgery
Nutrition 2	Severe weight loss – increased risk of complications post operatively. Care needed with calculation on anaesthetic and check on electrolytes which may require treatment to come into correct range	Explanation to patient May need to admit earlier to build up weight

Feature of number of underlying conditions such as cancer |

Characteristic	Problem	Issues
Smoking	Increases anaesthetic risk and risk of developing respiratory infection post operatively	May be required to give up smoking pre operatively and take bronchodilating medication to assist with reduction of post op risks
Oral Contraceptives	Can be associated with development of deep vein thrombosis and pulmonary embolism – serious and potentially fatal consequences	Often recommend stop taking for one month pre surgery
Cardiac or respiratory conditions	Increased risk of problems with anaesthetic or developing cardiac or respiratory problems post operatively	May need physiotherapy pre and post op. Asthmatics requiring steroids may require increase in dose to compensate. Patients with cardiac valve disease or having had replacement in past – may need antibiotic cover to ensure infective endocarditis does not occur.
Diabetes	Control of blood sugar problem in surgery due in part to lack of food and fluid. Can be serious problem where insulin dependant with potentially fatal consequences if not controlled adequately. Uncontrolled diabetics carry increased risk of infection and other postoperative complications.	Will need infusion with glucose and insulin Frequent blood sugar levels Unstable diabetics should be admitted for a few days pre operatively to have diabetes controlled. Usually urine specimens for glucose on admission. Even diabetics controlled by diet will require some attention although they may not require admission few days pre operatively.

Characteristic	Problem	Issues
Medications	Some medications can cause problems either during or post surgery. (See oral contraceptives)	MAOI anti depressants – discontinue if possible two weeks pre surgery Diuretics – even potassium sparing ones often result in reduction of potassium in blood. Potassium levels are important for the effective and safe use of anaesthetic. May require supplements as a result. Will require blood levels to be checked pre operatively and may need supplements for some days before surgery can take place. Cardiac medication particularly anti hypertensives should be checked carefully and may require modification or reduction in dosage before surgery. Steroids often need to be increased pre operatively.
Allergies and adverse drug reactions	Can lead to anaphylaxis – potentially fatal consequence of severe allergic reaction	All allergies should be detailed including penicillin-based antibiotics (common), narcotic analgesics and even plasters. Allergies can also be noted from blood transfusions. Particular care needed with any blood products. Need to rule out previous allergies to anaesthetics or any family history of anaesthetic problems.
Previous surgery	Complications in the past	Often recur.

4. Assessment – from examination and investigation

This assessment is completed by both the surgeon and the anaesthetist.

These assessments will be recorded in all except the most minor of surgical procedures and will be detailed in the medical records:

- Baseline observations – to check against during and post operation:–
  Pulse
  Blood pressure
  Temperature
  Respirations
  (See normal ranges)
- Weight
- Blood count – full blood count including haemoglobin levels
  – Check biochemistry – urea and electrolyte levels
  – Check blood group
- Urine and sputum specimens may be needed
- Chest x-ray unless very minor procedure
- ECG

5. Consent form

The consent form has to be signed by a parent or a guardian for a minor.

The surgical procedure should be explained by a member of the surgical team (in practice this is often a junior member).

The form should be a signed and dated version and be present before nursing staff will transfer the patient to the theatre. The form should be signed by both doctor and patient.

6. Pre operative care: (Nursing care)

See Pre Operative Checklist for specific items to check immediately pre transfer

- Fasting – Nil BY MOUTH – depends in nature of operation as to how long.

- Bowel preparation for GI surgery – enema or rectal washout (see Investigations and Procedures)
- Prophylactic care for thrombosis development – anti embolitic stockings (encourage flow of blood through veins in legs) and sometimes heparin given subcutaneously
- Shaving of area if necessary
- Pre medication
- Wristband
- Medical records collected for transfer
- X-ray films collected for transfer to theatre
- False teeth removed
- Make up and nail varnish removed
- Jewellery removed with exception of wedding ring, which should be taped over
- Check consent form signed.

Peri Operative Records: (during surgery)

1. Anaesthetic records
2. Swab and blood count

Personnel

The team is made up of:–

a. Anaesthetist

b. Operating theatre Assistant – does variety of tasks including assist anaesthetist and ensure correct placement of patient on table.

c. Surgeon – gowned

d. Surgical assistants – junior members of medical team – gowned

e. Perfusionist – cardiac surgery – maintains the flow of blood through a machine while surgery on the heart takes place. Perfusion equipment takes over the role of the heart.

f. Radiologist – can be called from time to time (particularly where orthopaedic operations are concerned – i.e.: to check bones placed correctly after trauma)

g. Scrub nurse – main nurse in charge of handing instruments to surgeon – gowned

h. Runner – nurse or operating theatre assistant who undertakes routine tasks such as collecting items needed for surgery (Types of sutures etc)

i. Nurse assistant – counting blood loss and ensuring (with scrub nurse) that correct amount of instruments are retained at end of surgery, no swabs left in place.

The Hazards of Surgery

Area	Problem	Avoidance
Eyes	Damage by mask and skin anaesthetics	Tape over unless ophthalmic surgery
Teeth	Damage from intubation and insertion of laryngoscope (instrument which allows for the insertion of the endotracheal tube into the windpipe)	False teeth removed pre operatively Caps and loose teeth noted pre op so anaesthetist aware of which at risk
Skin	Pressure sores	Table surface well padded Lengthy operation may use ripple mattress which alternates the area of pressure Pre op assessment of heavy or very thin patients – awareness of additional risks
Nerves	Compression or traction can lead to damage	Most common brachial plexus – where arm is extended and injury occurs in shoulder. Arm should not be allowed to fall below the level of the table. Where possible arm should be tucked at side of body. Where intravenous drip in progress armrest should be used to support arm. NB: *great care needed with the trendelenberg position* *Also: Common peroneal nerve at risk in lithotomy position*
Circulation and blood Blood transfusion	Incompatibility	Ensure correct type of blood or product is used

Area	Problem	Avoidance
Thrombosis (clot)	Results from compression and inactivity	Can use stimulators during long operations Anti embolitic stockings used Subcutaneous heparin can be given
Embolism of air	Air enters veins causing right side of heart to develop problems	Great care with cardiovascular and pulmonary surgery Ensure intravenous infusions set up and continued properly If occurs needs to be removed by aspiration as soon as possible. Increased risk with head and neck surgery.
Temperature	Control more difficult Hypothermia:	Anaesthetic prevents body from self regulation of temperature Hypothermia can develop (Lowering of central or core body temperature to dangerous level) Maintain room heat of theatre Maintain fluid balance Adequate covers (subject to surgical requirements) Blood warmed Aluminium foil (survival) blankets as necessary Particularly problem with burns patients
	Hyperthermia	Occasionally patients develop hyperpyrexias during surgery (excessive high temperature) Family history may be relevant. Where patient has temperature pre operatively and is pre medicated with atropine there is an increased risk.

Area	Problem	Avoidance
Tourniquets	Restrict or cut of blood supply to limb causing damage	Shortest period of time in use Usually more than 2 hours Care needed to check state and condition of limb during operation Times of application and removal carefully noted.
Electrical problems	Diathermy used (means of cauterising blood vessels to prevent bleeding, can also cut through some tissues). Anaesthetised patient does not react to burns	Plate which acts as electrode must be sited correctly.

The Operation note

The operation note details the operation although it is usually written immediately after the operation.

Contents

- Which surgeon and who assisted
- Position on table
- Incision used
- Procedure
- What found or removed
- How closed wound – suture or clip types
- Drains used
- Blood or fluid replacement and loss.
- Postoperative requirements

Position on operating table

(May also be described in the anaesthetic records).

a. Trendelenberg

Trendelenberg is used in pelvic surgery.

The position is for the head to be down and the feet to be upward.

N.B.: excessive tilt can cause problems because shoulder rests may dig in and damage the brachial plexus.

b. Lithotomy

Lithotomy is used in gynae surgery where the legs are placed in stirrups.

N.B.: As strain can be placed on lumbar spine must check pre operatively that hips and lumbar spine mobile enough.

c. Prone

This is lying on the front so the back is exposed.

N.B.: poor position for ventilation and abdominal compression can result.

d. Lateral

On the side.
N.B.: lower lung may not inflate as well.
Compression of limbs underneath body can be problem.
Nerve damage can be caused in lower arm.

e. Supine

On the back. This position is the most common.

N.B.: Lengthy operations can result with pressure on the sacrum and back of shoulders.

Incisions

Usually described according to the area affected. However there are a number of abdominal incisions used depending on the requirements of the surgeon and the condition being treated:

Abdominal incisions

- Right paramedian: (laparotomy)
- Gridiron (appendicectomy)

- Midline (laparatomy)
- Pfannensteil (pelvic surgery, caesarean and hysterectomy)
- Loin incision (Kidney surgery)
- Left lower paramedian (Bowel surgery)
- Sub costal (Kocher's incision) cholecystectomy – removal of gall bladder

Regions of the Abdomen

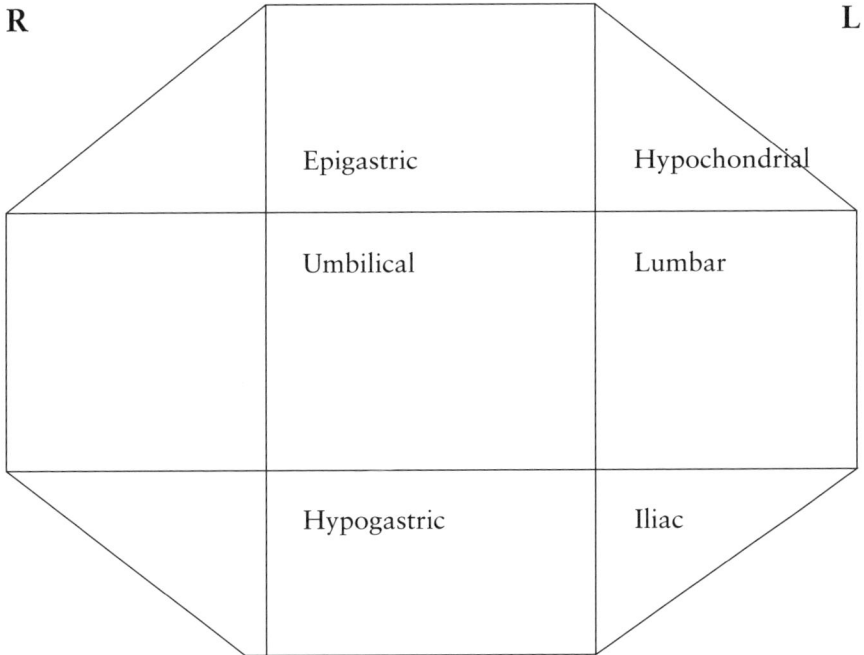

R   L

Epigastric	Hypochondrial
Umbilical	Lumbar
Hypogastric	Iliac

Incision Sites

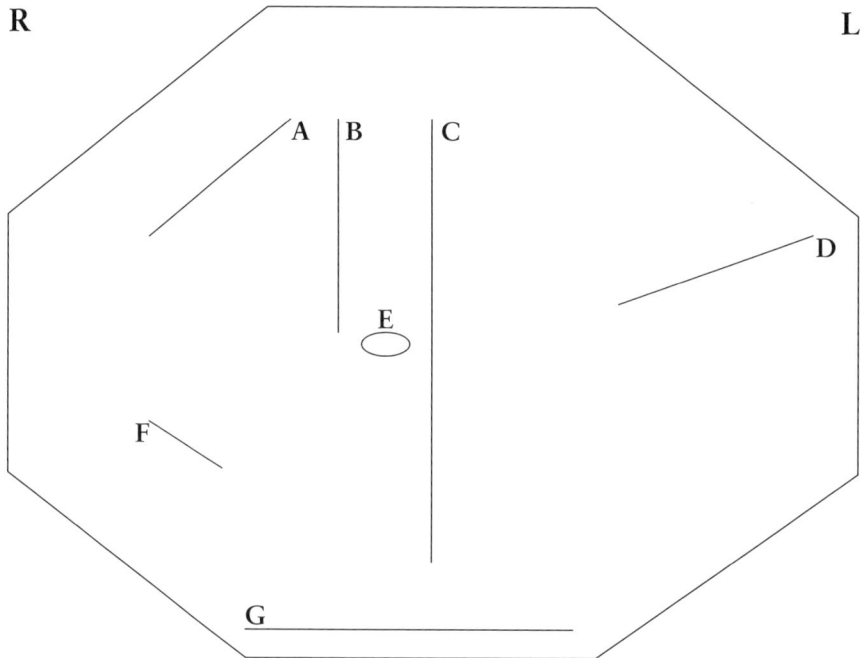

A	KOCHER'S SUB COSTAL	(Cholecystectomy)
B	RIGHT PARAMEDIAN	(laparotomy)
C	MIDLINE	(laparotomy)
D	LOIN	(renal)
E	UMBILICUS	
F	GRIDIRON	(appendicectomy)
G	PFANNENSTIEL	(gynaecological and pelvic surgery

Operation Note

These should record in detail the exact manner in which the operation was carried out and what if anything was removed or found. Any procedure should be detailed.

The note should detail who did the operation and who assisted the operation. Closure techniques should also be identified and detailed.

Sutures: – absorbable or non absorbable

Absorbable – disappear over time

Organic types such as
E.g.: catgut – either plain or chromic
    Plain – General control of bleeding in small vessels
    Chromic – general control of bleeding particularly in infected
    wounds
    Often used in biliary, gastrointestinal, genital, urinary and
    respiratory tract

Synthetic types
E.g.: Polyglycolic acid
    Polyglactin
    Dexon
    Vicryl

Similar uses to chromic catgut, stronger and possibly more reliable

Non-absorbable sutures

Organic – multi filament natural fibres
- Silk   Wide range of uses in non-infected tissues. Usually contra indicated in infected tissues
Replaced by synthetics to large degree
- Linen   General use where strong firm tie needed. Otherwise replaced by synthetics
- Cotton   Similar to silk but rarely used

Synthetic
- Monofilament polymers
- Multifilament polymers

Monofilament:
- Polymide: (Nylon, Dermalon and Ethilon)
Can be used in infected area and suitable for wide range of sutures.
- Polypropylene (Prolene, Surgilene)
Often used in cardiovascular surgery
- Polyethylene (Dermalene)
Often used in skin, tendons and cardiovascular surgery

Multi filament:
- Polymer – (Surgilon, Nurilon)
  Good for infected wounds and contaminated tissues
  General use
- Polyester (Dacron, Ethiflex)
  Used where strength is important
  Tendon repair, ophthalmic surgery and cardiovascular surgery
- Wires:
  used in cardiac surgery. Strong but breakable.

Swab Count and Blood Loss Records (Peri-operative Record)

These records are maintained by nursing or operating assistant staff.

The nurse records the instruments in the pack(s) (double counts with scrub nurse) and all instruments are returned to the pack. The nursing staff count all packets of swabs opened and used. The scrub nurse and general nurse will count all swabs returned from use and collected.

Blood loss can be recorded via suction i.e. the machine which sucks up fluid in the cavity. It can also be recorded by weight difference between unused swab or bandage and one soaked with blood.

Accurate records are essential so that effective replacement of fluids can be ensured.

The anaesthetist or operating theatre assistant will usually deal with replacement fluids in surgery i.e. blood or other infusions. These will be in the anaesthetic records and a total will usually be recorded in the operation note.

The Post Operative Period

Detailed in:

- The recovery records
- Nursing kardex on return to the ward
- Nursing care plan
- Clinical records

The Recovery records

The recovery records detail the immediate post-operative period until the patient is stable and breathing satisfactorily either on his own or with the assistance of ventilation.

They are usually in the form of an observations chart, or a kardex – noting any medications given and the route of administration; confirmation that the wound and drains are satisfactory; and a checklist to ensure all details are checked before patient is transferred to the ward or ITU.

Post operative: Risks and complications

These are the issues, which will be considered in the medical, and nursing records in the postoperative period.

Immediate concerns

After any general anaesthetic and surgical intervention there are initially three matters, which need to be considered in the recovery room:

a. Airway – The airway will need to be patent and clear

b. Breathing – regular, reasonable rate and no difficulty

c. Circulation – blood flow is satisfactory. No haemorrhage or leaking

More specifically the following are usually completed in the recovery room and when returned to the ward:

- Pulse
- Respirations
- Temperature (although may not be checked frequently)
- Blood pressure
- Wound site inspected – for leaking
- Drains – inspected for patency and flow
- Patient monitored for pain

Where specific types of surgery are undertaken there may be additional concerns and further or more frequent checks may be made:

Cardiac

- Haemorrhage and shock – some form of IV access necessary for the rapid input of fluids if required. Usually two forms of access although they may be through the one vein. Allows for intravenous fluids and specific medications (such as adrenaline) to be given in injection form.
- Embolism/thrombosis – check legs (signs of redness, swelling or heat), breathing (difficulty in breathing)
- Arrhythmias – place on cardiac monitor. Arrhythmias are common after cardiac surgery. Some are in the form of minor uncomfortable arrhythmias such as atrial fibrillation (where the top section of the heart on both side vibrates quickly and irregularly). Some can be more serious – ventricular tachycardia, ventricular fibrillation.
- Leg injury – coronary artery by pass grafts usually involve the removal of the saphenous vein from the leg and placing it within the heart to by pass the particular coronary arteries which are blocked. As a result there will be a long wound (often the length of the leg) and there is a risk of injury to the circulation of the leg. Pedal (foot) pulses should be checked. The leg should also be checked for signs of swelling or oedema (collection of fluid).

Pulmonary surgery

- Possibility of obstruction, atelectasis (collapse of the lung) and pneumonia (inflammation of the lung)
- Patients are often turned every few hours to avoid – depends on surgery and requirements of surgeon.

- Suction may be required, this involves the brief insertion of a narrow tube into the throat either via the mouth or nose to remove mucus and other substances, which could cause blockage.
- Pulmonary patients may also need humidified Oxygen (oxygen passed through water).
- Specialist physiotherapists will commence exercises but nurses may continue with more frequent work to keep lungs clear.

Neurological surgery
- Neurological observations should be undertaken at frequent intervals.
- Care should be taken to check for signs of restlessness, anxiety and fatigue

Genito urinary surgery
- Fluid input and output is particularly important.
- Possibility that patient will go into retention (become unable to pass urine)
  Check bladder to see if distended
- Most GU patients will have a catheter in place and output should be recorded as should colour and constituency

Gastro intestinal surgery
- Risk of intestinal tract becoming paralysed. PARALYTIC ILEUS.
- Most patients will remain NIL BY MOUTH for some days until BOWEL SOUNDS are heard. These are signs of flatus (wind) or the actual passing of stools. This indicates that the intestine is working and the gradual re introduction of food can be commenced.

General Post Operative Complications

Problem	Type	Treatment/ Investigation	Issues
Haemorrhage	Early post op	Depends on cause – often need to return to surgery	Poor haemostasis (regular control of blood), clotting problems
	Secondary	Blood for M C & S Antibiotics and surgery	Often infection related
Wound	Infection	Wound swab for M C & S. Temperature, pulse and respirations. Antibiotics and anti-pyrexials (reduce temperature)	May need surgery to remove any dead tissue and clean wound if serious infection
	Breakdown	Wound swab for M C & S. Temperature, pulse and respirations. Antibiotics and anti-pyrexials (reduce temperature) May need to be resutured	Depends on cause – often infection and poor blood supply
	Haematoma (clot)	Remove – some resolve over time without intervention	Large or multiple haematomas – check clotting of blood
Urinary system	Retention – failure to pass urine	Monitor input and output of patient – fluid balance chart. Try running water/standing patient up. If no success catheter passed	More common in elderly men
	Infection	Specimen if possible for M C & S Antibiotics	More common in women
Respiratory system	Infection	May need chest x-ray Specimen if possible Antibiotics	Physiotherapy may be required

Problem	Type	Treatment/ Investigation	Issues
	Aspiration Pneumonia Inflammation of the lungs due to aspiration of fluids	Specimen for M C & S Chest x-ray May require suction and re introduction of the endo tracheal tube (tube into the windpipe to assist with breathing) Antibiotics and steroids	Should not occur where adequate pre operative care provided and Nil by Mouth for 4–8 hours pre operatively
	Atelectasis (collapses of part of the lung due usually to obstruction by of the windpipe or bronchus by mucus	Suction, Chest x-ray, Chest drain depending on cause, bronchoscopy if severe, reintroduction of endo tracheal tube to assist with respiration. Arterial blood gases analysis and sputum specimen for M C & S. Pulse, respiration and importantly temperature. Antibiotics	Severe cases warrant urgent treatment and possibly further surgery. Mild cases may resolve with anti pyrexials and assistance with nebulisers to dilate the bronchials Good physiotherapy often of assistance
Gastro intestinal system	Paralytic Ileus (Paralysed gastric system – no movement)	Examination – abdominal distension No bowel sounds Vomiting present Abdominal x-ray If severe problem pass NG (naso gastric tube) and aspirate (remove contents) frequently. Intravenous infusion to maintain hydration Antibiotics if infection present Bloods for urea and electrolytes to check all electrolytes in correct range. If not will require some correction to ensure no further problems arise	Most Paralytic ileus associated with gastric and abdominal surgery. Usually settle within a few days. If do not settle possiblity of some form of obstruction and exploratory surgery may be required.

Problem	Type	Treatment/ Investigation	Issues
Cerebral difficulties	Confusion	Full blood count Chest x-ray Biochemistry for urea and electrolytes, urine and sputum specimens for M C & S, Blood gases, glucose levels and if no other cause found – CT scan	More common with the elderly

Infection

By far the most common of postoperative problems relates to the development of infection. This can be local infection within the wound or more systemic as a result of infection developing in one system and spreading throughout the body.

Increasingly the medical profession are becoming wary of widespread use of antibiotics because of the development of strains of bacteria, which are resistant to common antibiotics. The MRSA (known as either multi or methicillin resistant staphylococcus aureus) for example may result in a ward being closed to admissions while the MRSA is eradicated. In an elderly or vulnerable individual MRSA can be fatal. It can develop into a serious infection, which is difficult to treat.

It is almost impossible in any hospital for MRSA to be completely removed. However once detected it should be possible for MRSA to be contained. The most common form of transmission of infection is generally thought to be the medical profession itself, failing to wash hands between examination and treatment of patients.

Despite the concerns of the medical profession there are some forms of surgery where prophylactic antibiotics are generally considered appropriate. Some forms of abdominal or orthopaedic surgery will usually include antibiotics in the postoperative care regime. Traumatic accidents particularly where the wounds are unclean will usually warrant antibiotics due to the high risk of infection developing.

Prophylactic antibiotics

- *Coliform organisms* – common in gastic, bilary and genito urinary surgery –
  Cephalosporin
- *Anaerobic organisms* – common in lower gastro intestinal and abdominal surgery –
  Metronidazole
- *Staphylococci* (usually aureus) – common in vascular and orthopaedic surgery (insertion of prostheses) –
  Flucloxacillin or cephalosporin
- *Tetanus infection* – common in dirty or infected wounds
  Penicillin
- *Streptococci* – common or high risk in dental procedures, which can lead to infective endocarditis (infection of the endometrium of the heart – a serious condition)
  Amoxycillin with or without (depending on risk)
  Vancomycin and Gentamycin

Final Post operative considerations

Detailed in the medical and nursing records:

- Removal of sutures or clips
- Discharge medication
- Removal of drains, infusions
- Confirmation pulse, blood pressure and temperature are stable
- Information on postoperative exercise and diet
- Clinic appointments
- Physiotherapy appointments and exercises
- Information on any signs which warrant return to hospital or the GP
- Letter to GP to confirm procedure and progress
- Discharge by nurses to community care – GP or community nursing staff

Medical records – the pre operative care plan – Nursing

Problem	Goal	Plan	Evaluation
Fred is anxious	To reassure and allow him to express concerns	a. allow time to discuss concerns with Fred b. encourage him to express worries c. explain procedures	*Discussed with Fred. Anaesthetist and surgeon have explained*
Fred needs to be prepared for surgery	To be prepared	Pre operative check list to be completed Ensure Fred understands nature of procedure Washout to be day pre surgery Gown in place TED stockings in place Pre medication as scripted	*Consent form signed Pre op check list complete. BO with good effect* *Teds in place and pre med – omnapon IM given @ 10:00*
Fred will be Nil by mouth per operatively	To be comfortable	Ensure mouth wash available Sign on bed to ensure no fluids or food by mouth Ensure Fred understands why	*NBM form midnight* *Mouth washes PRN*

Keys:

BO	bowels opened	IM	Intramuscular injection
Teds	type of stockings which help to prevent blood clots forming in legs	NBM PRN Omnapon	nil by mouth as needed pre medication

Immediate post operative care plan – Nursing

Problem	Goal	Plan	Evaluation
Fred will be unable to maintain his airway	To ensure breathing is satisfactory	Check patency of airway Oxygen 2L	*Breathing without assistance Resps good*
Fred is at risk of bleeding	To avoid haemorrhage To detect bleeding	Check wound site Record output of blood into drains Pulse and blood pressure at 15 min intervals	*Wound site satisfactory Draining 10-30 mls per hour Obs ok*
Fred may have pain post operatively	To be comfortable and to deny pain	Ensure Fred reports pain Medication as scripted Look for non verbal signs of pain	*Nil report of pain IM Omnapon given @ 14:00*

Keys:

Resp   respiratory rate
Obs   Pulse temperature and blood pressure
2l   Two litres

Longer term post operative care plan – Nursing

Problem	Goal	Plan	Evaluation
Fred has an infected wound	To treat infection and maintain clean wound	Wound swab for M C & S Antibiotics as scripted Dressing BD N/saline Temperature QDS	Swab ✓ Abx as scripted IVI discontinued BD Dressings - wound appears clean Apyrexial Sutures removed - wound now ok
Fred has a chest infection	To treat and make Fred comfortable	Sputum for M C & S Antibiotics Obs QDS Encourage production of sputum Oxygen PRN	Sputum ✓ Obs ✓ Producing quantity of yellow sputum O2 PRN Chest physio given with good effect
Fred is not mobile	To avoid risks of non mobility	Passive limb exercises TEDs to remain in situ Heparin as scripted Ensure mobile in bed Laxatives PRN Increase fluids Increase fibre in diet	Passive limb exercises ✓ Teds in situ Fybogel given with good effect Fluids increased

Keys:

Abx	antibiotics	O2	oxygen
IVI	intravenous infusion	TEDs	stocking which help prevent clots forming

BD   twice a day

QDS   four times a day

PRN   as needed

Fybogel   encourages bowels to
           open by passing fibre
           through intestine

Neurology

Neurology

The Neurological system: Anatomy and Physiology

This book does not aim to provide a detailed analysis of the role and work of the neurological system.

As a basic summary however, nerves are pathways throughout the body which transmit either messages or impulses. Some nerves are involved with movement (**Motor/Efferent Nerves**) and some with the senses (**Sensory/Afferent Nerves**).

The neurological system can be roughly divided into the following areas:

a. central nervous system – i.e. the brain and spinal cord
b. the peripheral nervous system being:

    i.   31 pairs of spinal nerves
    ii.   12 pairs of cranial nerves
    iii. the autonomic nervous system

The Central Nervous System

The central nervous system includes the cerebrum (which is the larger part of the brain and is made up of a number of lobes), the brain stem and the cerebellum which is the hind or back brain. It also includes the spinal cord which is a long section of the central nervous system running the length of most of the back. It is surrounded by CSF (**cerebrospinal fluid**). The job of CSF is to protect the brain and spinal cord, keep an even pressure around those structures, keep them moist and act as a cushion.

The spinal cord is the link between the brain and the rest of the body. The nerves go through the spinal cord and depart at the appropriate level in pairs to the organs or tissues. The spinal cord itself ends at the upper lumbar level although nerves spread out from the bottom section through to the lower sections of the body. This area is known as the **cauda equina** because it resembles a horse's tail.

The Peripheral Nervous System

i. Spinal Nerves

All the way along the spinal cord there are a number of nerves which lead off in pairs from different levels. These are known as the spinal nerves. Their names are related to their position and the vertebrae (bones of the spine) to which are near.

There are therefore:

8	cervical spinal nerves
12	thoracic
5	lumbar
5	sacral
1	coccygeal

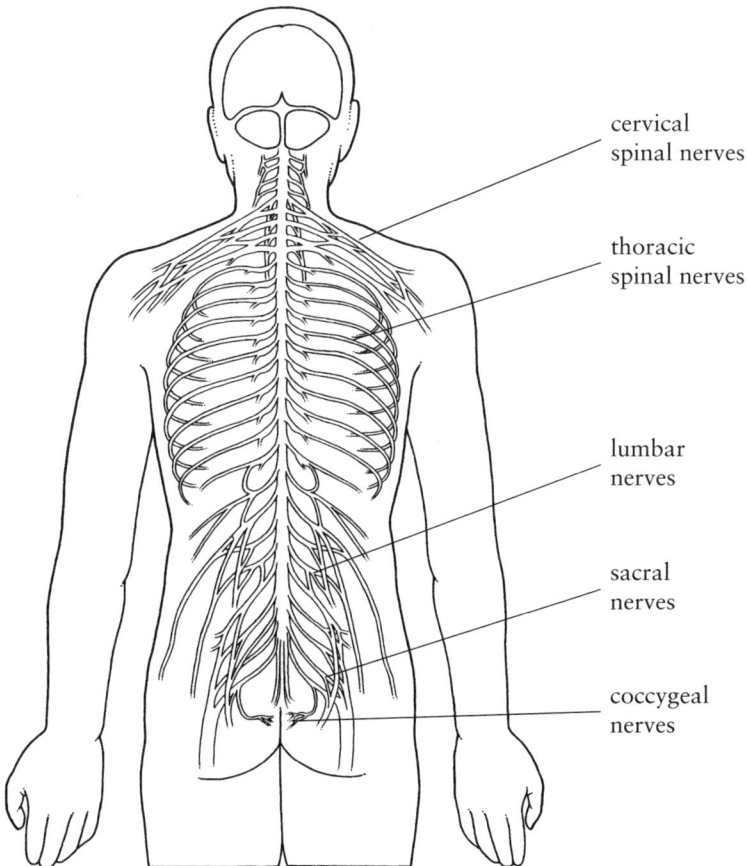

The lumbar, sacral and coccygeal nerves form part of the cauda equina. Each nerve includes a motor and sensory element. They are often referred to as **mixed nerves**.

The nerves which divide off from the spinal cord in some cases collect together before separating off to their specific areas. These groupings of nerves are called the **Plexuses**. There are five large groupings:

- Cervical plexus – supplies nerves which relate to the neck, sternum and diaphragm
- Brachial plexus – skin and muscles of arm and chest.
- Lumbar plexus – the femoral (upper section of leg), thigh and trunk
- Sacral plexus – muscles of pelvis, hip joint, pelvic organs and the sciatic nerve
- Coccygeal plexus – skin in coccyx and pelvic floor muscles

The thoracic nerves supply the chest and some of the muscles of the abdomen.

ii. The Cranial Nerves

The cranial nerves are the nerves originating in the brain which control various aspects of the movement of the face or sensory detection.

Some are both and therefore **Mixed**.

Nerve	Name	Type	Function
I	Olfactory	Sensory	Smell
II	Optic	Sensory	Vision
III	Oculomotor	Motor	Vision
IV	Trochlear	Motor Sensory	Vision Cornea
V	Trigeminal	Motor	Chewing
VI	Abducens	Motor	Vision
VII	Facial	Sensory Motor	Taste Expression
VIII	Vestibulocochlear	Sensory	Balance and equilibrium
IX	Glossopharangeal	Sensory Motor	Taste Swallowing
X	Vagus	Sensory Motor	Pharynx Vocal
XI	Accessory	Motor	Shoulders
XII	Hypoglossal	Motor	Tongue and Surrounding structures

For each pair of nerves there are tests which can be undertaken (usually during examination) which will demonstrate whether there is a problem or whether the nerves themselves are intact.

iii. Autonomic Nervous System

This system controls those activities which are completed automatically, such as changes in rate of heart beat, secretion of saliva and control of bladder function.

For ease the autonomic system is considered to be divided into two:

a. Sympathetic nervous system
b. Parasympathetic nervous system

The sympathetic nervous system has a general effect of preparation of the body for activity, excitement, fear and stress.

The parasympathetic nervous system is the more calming system, restoring matters to the pre-excitement levels. It is usually associated with slowing down the body systems except in digestion or genito urinary systems.

Examination: the basics

Neurological examination can be lengthy and complex depending on the reason for the referral and the suspected cause of any problems. It involves not just an examination of the person as they present, but also of the nerves – both the cranial nerves (for which there are detailed tests in themselves) and the peripheral nerves.

Whilst other specialities can to some extent rely on a battery of tests for their diagnosis, in many cases the examination in neurology may be the sole means by which a potential diagnosis can be reached. For this reason the examination procedure is provided in some depth.

Appearance and behaviour

- Neglect   – *possible depression, addiction*
- Depressed
- Anxious
- Aggressive behaviour or over familiar
- Crying or laughing easily   – *Labile*
- Unresponsive   – *flat affect*

Testing memory

a. Orientation

Check whether individual can confirm the following:

- Time – day, date, month, year, time of year, time of day
- Place – city, street, hospital or clinic, area of country
- Person – name, job, where live, family

b. Memory

- Immediate test – check whether can remember information immediately minor information with some detail e.g. an address
- Short term – check whether can recall details in five minutes
- Long term – life events, football team members of team supported by individual

c. Abstract thought

- Usually finishing proverbs
  Test for frontal lesions and dementia
- Ask to explain differences between items (cat and dog for example)

d. Calculations

- Simple then increasingly complex calculations

Spatial awareness

- Relatively complex diagram such as house or clock face, inability to draw *possible constructional weakness* – known as constructional apraxia.
  Apraxia
- Inability to perform a task
  Imaginary task – tossing a pancake, buttoning a shirt
  If does but with errors – *ideomotor apraxia*
  If can not do i.e. understands task but cannot perform – *ideational apraxia*

Visual and body perception

- Uses all limb appropriately
- Place item in hand and see if can guess contents – with eyes shut.

Examination of the Cranial Nerves

Olfactory Nerve (I)

Checks deal with smell:–

- If individual can smell reasonable variety common smells and identify correctly – normal
- If can only smell ammonia regardless
- If anosmia on both sides – possibility psychological difficulties

Optic Nerve and the Eye (II)

This examination checks:–

- **Pupils** – check react to light
- **Acuity** – can be affected by cataracts and other ophthalmic problems
- **Fields** – can be normal. Defects are extremely useful in identifying the position of a lesion
- **Fundi** – the interior of the eye

Ophthalmic terms are not in common usage and can be more difficult to translate from the structure of the words. Common terms used in neurological examination include the following:

Term	Meaning
Homonymous	Defect at same part of field in both eyes
Congrous	Matches exactly
Incongrous	Does not match
Ptosis	Drooping eyelid
Exophthalmus	Protrusion of the eye
Enophthalmus	Sunken eye
Aniscoria	Pupils unequal but reactive
Meiosis	Contraction of pupil
RAPD	Relative afferent papillary defect also known as Marcus Gunn pupil – one sided lesion
Horners syndrome	Small pupils react to light but have drooping eyelid and enophthalmus (see above)
Hemianopia	Loss of sight in half of visual field
Scotoma	Hole in visual field
Quadrantanopias	Defects in particular quadrant of vision
Papilloedema	Excess fluid or swelling of the optic disc often due to increased pressure within the skull – raised intra cranial pressure
Papillitis	Inflammation of the optic disc

Checks: Pupils

- Symmetry – particularly of eyelid
- Position of eye
- Size and equality of pupil
- Reactiveness to light
- Shine light in one eye – check for reflex (DIRECT REFLEX)
- Shine light in other eye but check first eye (CONSENSUAL REFLEX)

The NORMAL reaction is where the pupil constricts with the light. Where one side constricts and other dilates it is a one sided lesion known as RAPD. This could be caused by inflammation of the optic nerve or compression on the nerve.

Horner's syndrome is often caused by stroke or trauma.

Checks: Acuity

- Use chart
- Use normal material such as book

Problems could be age related, cataract formation, inflammation of the optic nerve or many other causes.

Checks: Fields

- Place hands outstretched and move fingers on one hand
- Check from individual which hand is moving
- Test each eye individually
- Move pin or small object in arc shape movement. Individual to confirm when it appears to be red.

Term	Defect	Possible cause
Tubular vision	Constricted field stays same size even when object is at some distance	Suggestive of psychological problems
Scotoma	Hole in visual field	Multiple sclerosis Damage to optic nerve Reduction in blood supply to retina
Altitudinal defects	Visual restriction either at top or bottom of field	Vascular cause
Homonymous hemianopias	Defects in same half of vision/field	Lesion site varies
Homonymous Quadrantanopias	Defect same quadrant of vision	Upper field could be temporal lobe lesion Lower field could be parietal lobe lesion

- One eye – scotoma, altitudinal defect and tubular vision
- Both eyes – quandrantanopias and homonymous hemianopias

Checks: Fundi

The fundi is the interior of the eye behind the lens and the pupil. It is generally examined by the ophthalmoscope (equipment shining different lights into the eye). In checking – review the optic disc (small part of the retina which is white coloured)

- Check the blood vessels
- Check that they have a pulse
- Check the optic disc – if the disc cannot be seen but the patient has normal sight – suspect *papilloedema* (swelling of optic nerve due to increased pressure).

If the optic disc cannot be seen and the patient can see nothing – suspect papillitis – common cause: multiple sclerosis.

If the disc can be seen but the patient can see nothing, suspect neuritis (inflammation of the nerve).

Area	Signs	Possible condition	Issues
Optic disc	No disc Patient ok vision	Papilloedema	Serious condition
	No disc Patient ok vision	Papillitis – optic nerve inflammation	MS suspected
	Can see disc Patient no vision	Neuritis	
	Atrophy (wasting)	Suspect MS, optic nerve compression	Sometimes follow papilloedema
Blood vessels	Veins narrow where crosses artery	Arteriovenous nipping	High blood pressure damaging retina *Hypertensive retinopathy*
	New vessels near disc	Neo-(new) vascularisation	Long term complication of diabetes – damage to retina *Diabetic retinopathy*
	Yellow object in artery	Cholesterol	Forms clot and blocks blood supply
Retinal background	Small haemorrhages near blood vessels	Dot haemorrhages	Possible diabetic retinopathy
Retinal background	Bleeds in deeper layer of retina	Blot haemorrhages	As above
	Superficial bleed in fan shape pointing towards optic disc	Flame haemorrhage	Hypertensive retinopathy
	White or yellow lesions	Hard exudates	Diabetes complication Also high blood pressure
	Cotton wool spots	Soft exudates	Long term complication of diabetes
	Black lesions	Number of causes	Suspect melanoma until otherwise (tumour)

Oculomotor (III) Trochlear (IV) and Facial (Adducens) Nerves (VI)

Checks

- Eye movements
- Double vision – marked by a false and extra vision in the affected eye
- Ensure do not have squint
- Move pen up and down, side to side to check whether has double vision
- Check whether eyes move together and in time

Misalignment of eyes which is constant wherever looking – squint.

Misalignment where one deviates downwards – may be a nerve lesion on the third cranial nerve.

Consider the following if double vision present:

1. Images wide apart but parallel – possible problem with VI nerve

2. Images seen downwards and at an angle – possible IV nerve affected

3. Images in other directions, drooping eyelid present – III nerve may be affected

Position and development of double vision could indicate some form of lesion.

Trigeminal nerve (V) and the Facial Nerve (VII)

The Face: Checks

Examination –

- Normal in appearance
- Abnormal: for example Cushingoid (obese and round due to steroids)
- Symmetrical

Tasks:

- Check teeth

- Whistle
- Look at ceiling

Motor neurone disease can be indicated where facial muscles affected
Particularly where weakness is detected

Test of Trigeminal nerve: Checks

1. Push against hand stopping jaw opening
2. Open mouth and check with small hammer jaw movement
3. Muscles surrounding jaw – check not wasted
4. Check sensation of jaw
5. Check whether pain in area

Possible problems:

1–2. Jaw deviates to one side on opening – possible lesion of V nerve
3. Wasting could be due to Motor neurone disease
4. Loss of sensation could be due to lesion
5. Pain could be trigeminal neuralgia

Auditory nerve (VIII)

There are two tests, auditory and vestibular:

Auditory – Checks

- Test each ear separately
- If hearing reduced in one ear will need further tests
- Look for a *Rinne's test*
  Uses a tuning fork in different places – on the mastoid process (bone behind ear) and in front of the ear. If hear better when on mastoid process – conductive deafness.
    If hears better when in front of ear – sensorineural deafness.
- Look for a *Weber's test* –
  Use a tuning fork on crown of head – if hears better in deaf ear – has conductive deafness
    If hears better in good ear – has sensorineural deafness (hearing loss due to lesion in inner ear or 8th nerve).

N.B. Importance: treated differently and with different causes

- Conductive – obstruction or middle ear disease
- Sensorineural – lesions in inner ear or 8th nerve caused by possible meningitis, sclerosis, drug or noise induced damage

Vestibular: Checks

- Gait – typical types – walking

Appearance	Symmetrical	Type	Common cause
Small shuffling	Yes	Parkinsonian	Parkinsons disease Major tranquillisers
Normal size but uncoordinated	No veers towards one side	Cerebellar ataxia A disorder of the brain causing irregular actions	Drugs. Alcohol, multiple sclerosis Problems with blood supply in brain
Normal but rotating shoulders and pelvis	Not necessarily	Waddling	Weak muscles Congenital dislocation of hip
Looks as if does not know how to walk, frequently stops	No	Apraxic	Hydrocephalus (extra fluid in brain) Problems with blood supply in brain
Crosses legs over, toes dragged on floor	No	Scissoring	Cerebral palsy Multiple sclerosis
Leg swings out to one side	No	Hemiplegic	Stroke, multiple sclerosis
One knee lifts higher than other	No	Foot drop	Peroneal nerve damage Peripheral neuropathy (damage to the peripheral nerves)

Auditory nerve problems – veers to one side and unsteady

- Caloric testing:
  Lie patient down on pillow (30 degrees)
  Cool water poured into one ear
  Patient looks ahead and eyes examined
  Then redone with warn water
- Check for nystagmus
  (One eye slowly drifts in one direction while other eye drifts rapidly in other direction)
  Normally:–
  - Where cold water fast response would be away from ear
  - Where warm water fast response is towards ear

If one ear has reduced response to either – problem with ear such as Meniere's disease (diseases of inner ear causing giddiness) or nerve damage.

If reduced nystagmus in one direction when warm water in one ear and cold water in other, could be brainstem lesion or some form of vascular disease.

Glossopharyngeal (IX), Vagus (X) and Hypoglossal (XI)

Mouth Checks

- Check tongue does not deviate from side to side when out of mouth
- Check repeated movements
- Small tongue – with reduced movement – possible upper motor neurone lesion
- Small tongue – with formation of bundles or collection of fibres – possible lower motor neurone lesion
- Large tongue – possible congenital hypothyroidism (reduced working of the thyroid gland) or acromegaly (condition caused by problems with the pituitary glands resulting in large features, particularly facial).

Pharynx and gag reflex – Checks

- Check appearance
- Watch drinking

- Check UVULVA (small fleshy body hanging down from roof of mouth at back)
- Check gag reflex working properly
- Uvulva should move when gag reflex tried

If Uvulva does not move at all – problem with the muscles of the palate

If does not move with gag reflex – could be problem with IX nerve

Larnyx – checks

- Ask individual to cough
- Watch drinking
- Any problems with speech?

If bubbly voice or cough then tenth nerve lesion is a possibility.

If swallow with coughing soon after, then tenth nerve lesions possible.

Accessory nerve (XI)

Checks

- Muscles in neck – signs of wasting
- Shoulders – sign of wasting
- Symmetrical muscles – shrug of shoulders should demonstrate

Weakness on one side – peripheral accessory nerve problems

One sided delayed shrug on shoulder – upper motor neurone lesion

Wasting and weakness on both sides – myopathy (disease causing deterioration in muscle)

Other tests and examinations

1. Reflexes
2. Miscellaneous tests
3. Sensory
4. Motor
5. Glasgow coma scale
6. EEG and EMG

1. Reflexes

Name	Test	Issues	Medical records entry
Biceps	hands on abdomen – place finger on biceps tendon and hit with hammer	testing the musculocutaneous nerve (root C5/C6)	B
Supinator	arm across abdomen, place finger on radial tuberosity (area of wrist just down from the thumb)	unhelpful name – muscle involved is brachoradialis. Tests musculocutaneous nerve, root C6	S
Triceps	Arm across chest at 90 degrees, strike triceps tendon with hammer – outer section, just above elbow.	radial nerve. Nerve root C7 (C6 and C8)	T
Knee	Place hand behind knee so 90 degrees, strike knee below patella	Femoral nerve Root L3–4	K
Ankle	Variety of ways hold at 90 degrees and hit Achilles tendon	Tibial nerve Root S1–2	A
Plantar	Foot – stroke the underside of the foot	described in terms of flexion (toes curl) and extension (spread)	P

Other Reflexes

Reflex	Elicited by	Normal Response	Abnormal response
Babinski	Stroking sole of foot	Toes flex (curl)	Toes spread and big toe extends – positive sign (possible upper motor neurone lesion) No response as above
Chaddock	Stroking below the Lateral malleolus	Great toe fans out	Responses as above
Oppenheim	Thumb and index finger down middle of tibia	Great toe fans out	Responses as above
Kernig	Lie on bed Flex leg at hip with knee bent Try to extend knee	Pain along the posterior of the thigh Knee straightens without difficulty	Resistance to straightening – indicates irritation of the meninges (the membranes round the skull and brain) One side only – possible radiculopathy (disease of nerve roots)
Cremasteric	Inner aspect of thigh stroked downwards	Testicle on that side elevated	Absent – could be due to local surgery. Lesion above lumbar 1 disc
Palmo mental reflex	Scratch palm of hand and look at chin	No reaction	Contraction of muscle same side of chin – positive One sided indicates possible frontal lobe problems
Grasp reflex	Place fingers on palm and pull away asking individual to let go of hand	Able to let go	Involuntary grabs hand – more frequent where frontal lobe problems. One sides – suggestive of clear problems with frontal lobe

Grading System

Grade	Symbol	Interpretation
5	5+	Hyperactive (with clonus)
4	4+	Very brisk
3	3+	Brisk
2	2+	Normal (average)
1	1+	Diminished but present
0	0	Absent

Alternative recording of reflexes:

–   absent
+   present but depressed
++   normal
+++   increased

Description of plantar reflexes

↑   extensor
↓   flexor
↑↓   equivocal

Medical records: testing of reflexes

Reflex	Right	Left
B	++	++
S	++	++
T	++	++
K	++	++
A	++	++
P	↓	↓

2. Other tests

Tinel's Sign

Use of hammer at site of any compression. If the nerve attached to area produces paraesthesia (problems with feeling/numbness) positive sign. Problem with nerve. Common for wrist problems.

Straight leg raising

Test for nerve root entrapment
  Lying flat on bed lift leg and check whether can reach 90 degree angle. Elderly patients are unlikely to be able to do so normally. Note difference between two sides. Pain possibly due to nerve root entrapment.

3. Sensory problems

Sensory examination needs great care to ensure its results are accurate. Different areas of the body are affected by different nerves. A reasonable anatomy and physiology book will demonstrate in detail the area of influence for each nerve.

Area of sensation	Nerve
Thumb and first two fingers of hand	Median
Little finger and half next finger	Ulnar
Back of hand between thumb and first finger	Radial
Top outer side of arm	Axillary
Top outer aspect of thigh	Lateral cutaneous
Outer aspect of lower part of leg	Common peroneal
Inner thigh and lower leg	Femoral
Back of leg – particularly lower section	Sciatic

Check
- Light sensation
- Pinprick
- Temperature
- Vibration (using tuning fork)

The Motor System

Basic signs to consider

Pattern/problem	Sign 1	Sign 2	Sign 3
Upper motor neurone	Increase in tone	Brisk reflexes	Weakness
Psychological (functional) problems	No wasting	Normal tone and power	Odd distribution of symptoms
Muscle problems	Wasting	Decrease in tone	Absent reflexes
Lower motor neurone	Wasting	Decreased tone	Absent reflexes

Common patterns and possible causes

a. Weakness all limbs – no reflexes – damage to or disease of nerves

b. Arms and legs: mixture of lower motor neurone patterns and upper motor neurone patterns – suggests possible motor neurone disease

c. weakness in all limbs and increased reflexes – suggests spinal cord lesion in the neck or motor neurone disease

d. weakness in legs and increased reflexes – problem with spinal cord

e. weakness in legs no reflexes – problem with peripheral nerves

f. weakness and increased reflexes down one side of the body – probable stroke

Glasgow coma scale

Means by which can assess conscious state of patient.

- 15 – normal level of consciousness
- minimum possible score = 3

Eyes open:

Spontaneously	4
To verbal stimuli	3
To pain	2
Never	1

Best verbal response

Oriented and converses	5
Disoriented and converses	4
Inappropriate words	3
Incomprehensible words	2
No response	1

Best motor response

Obeys commands	6
Localise pain	5
Flexion (withdrawal to pain)	4
Abnormal flexion	3
Abnormal extension	2
No response	1

Total:

Summary of neurological assessment

- Gait
- Pupils PEARL – Pupils equal and reacting to light
- Fundi
- Eye movements
- Facial
- Neck
- Arms
- Legs
- Sensation

Other forms of testing

1. EEG

2. EMG

3. TENSILON TEST – injection of anticholinesterase to check diagnosis of myasthenia gravis (anticholinesterase inhibits the action of acetylcholine which transmits nerve impulses at certain sites within the nervous system).

Neurological Conditions

Disorders of consciousness

Temporary loss of consciousness:–

Epilepsy

This is a condition marked by abnormal electrical activity of the brain. Some people would appear to be more susceptible than others. Clinically epileptics are often divided into two artificial groups –

a. Idiopathic where there is no sign of organic disease and

b. Symptomatic where the signs of the disorder are related to some form of underlying condition.

Symptomatic conditions include trauma, tumours abscesses or degenerative brain disease. Idiopathic epilepsy is sometimes referred to as central or centrencephalic epilepsy.

In practice epilepsy often is classified according to the type of seizure. This can be done in one of two major ways:

Traditional

Focal epilepsy: (Partial or limited seizures)

Focal epilepsy is generally associated with some form of local lesion or trauma. Attacks vary and can include from short temporary loss of consciousness or minor impairment of consciousness to uncommonly lengthy attacks in which part of the face or limbs may be affected for some days. Depending on the site of the lesion or trauma the effects will vary.

Some disturbance near to the speech areas of the brain may result in speech problems:

Aphasia – lack of ability to speak
Dysphasia – difficulty in speaking

Generalised seizures

Petit mal
Otherwise known as absence seizures where the individual appears not to be quite with matters. Often appears asleep with eyes open. Always brief. Occasionally marked by jerking of the limbs.

Usually begin in childhood between five and 16 years of age. Rarely proceed past adolescence and prognosis for those who have no family history of seizures and appear to have a normal to good IQ.

EEG is characteristic and seizure can often be produced in clinic allowing for definitive diagnosis.

Diagnosis must be accurate because medication is condition specific.

Major seizures

Tonic and clonic attacks
These are the **Grand Mal** fits – serious and major attacks for which often no specific cause is found. The progress of a typical fit is as follows although these stages do not occur in every case:

- Aura – sense of warning for a few seconds before the fit starts
- Loss of consciousness and falling to ground
- Tonic phase – where muscles go rigid, the individual may appear blue (cyanosed) due to lack of oxygen, teeth are usually clenched and on occasions frothing at the mouth will be apparent
- Clonic phase – relaxation of the muscles with movement and jerking.
- Deep sleep or confusion. This varies from attack to attack but often the individual appears to be in a deep sleep but is

rousable albeit confused. On occasions they will suffer a headache for some time after the attack and may feel nauseous.

Alternative Analysis of Seizures

Partial Seizures

These begin with epileptic activity in a specific part of the brain. They are classified according to whether the person loses normal consciousness during the attack (complex partial seizures) or not (simple partial seizures).

Seizures may begin as partial seizures but spread to become generalised seizures.

Generalised Seizures

These are not localised to a specific area. There are many types: for example

- Absence seizures (also known as petit-mal) where the person appears not to be aware of their surroundings but usually do not twitch
- Tonic clonic seizures (also known as grand mal). The person loses consciousness often after a warning or aura that a fit is about to start. The tonic phase is a stiffening of the muscles and the clonic phase is jerking of the limbs.

Records may have either version of categorisation within them.

Pseudoseizures

These are seizures that appear to have no physical cause. These can be indicative of psychiatric disorder rather than epilepsy.

It can be difficult to differentiate between the two groups although if someone appears to have a grand mal fit but the EEG recording is normal they could be suffering from pseudo seizures.

Treatment

Petit mal attacks respond to specific medications.

Other forms of seizure respond to common anti epileptic medication.

Measurements of the amount of the particular medication in the blood are usually taken from time to time to ensure correct dosage.

Usual Drugs
1. Carbemazepine
2. Phenytoin
3. Sodium Valporate
4. Gabapentin
5. Lamotrigine

Note: A discussion should occur and be documented about the person's driving and work. If they have epilepsy they must not drive or operate heavy machinery and should inform the DVLC.

Other Neurological Conditions

Condition	Symptoms	Investigation	Issues
Bells palsy	Problems with facial muscles	Check ear and mouth to exclude herpes Cranial nerve check	Steroids may assist Often recover few weeks
Stroke CVA Often known as a cerebral vascular accident or attack	Weakness usually one sided (hemiplegia) Diplopia (double vision) Problems with speech	Resuscitation if needed White cell count Erythrocyte sedimentation rate Chest x-ray ECG Urinalysis CT scan	Conservative treatment and treatment of cause – hypertension (high blood pressure) speech therapy and rehabilitation
Parkinson's disease Slow progressive condition	Slow speech and poor movement Rigidity and tremor even at rest	No laboratory tests Clinical appearance	Levodopa, can be drug induced. May require surgery
MS multiple sclerosis	Relapse from time to time optic problems as nerves waste increasing difficulty with walking urinary symptoms vertigo and muscle problems	No single test. Electro-physiological studies can be helpful CT MRI scan Lumbar puncture	Progressive disease. Steroids may reduce the length of an attack
MND motor neurone disease	Progressive sporadic wasting gradually spreading causing weakness in speech and swallowing	Clinical appearance EMG	Progressive. Rare to survive more than 3 years
Myasthenia gravis	Weakness and fatigue	Tensilon test (One off bolus dose of anticholinesterase – improvement within seconds lasting few minutes – positive result)	Anticholinesterase medication and drugs with suppress the immune system Unknown cause

Typical records

25 yr woman	25 year old woman
c/o headache +++	Complaining of severe headache
↑ Temp	Increasing temperature
HPC 1/7 ↑ Temp	History of present complaint – one day history of increasing temperature
photophobia +++	Extreme photophobia
PMHx Nil of note	No past medical history
Shx student - Cardiff	Social history student at Cardiff
O/E neck stiffness, kernig +	On examination neck stiffness and a positive kernig sign
° rash	No rash
papilloedema ✓	Papilloedema present
↑ drowsiness	Increasing drowsiness
imp bacterial meningitis	Impression bacterial meningitis
FOR LP - CSF to C & S	Lumbar puncture with CSF to lab for culture and sensitivity tests
bloods U & E	Bloods to lab for urea and electrolyte studies
CXR and Head XR	Chest and head x-rays
CSF gram +ve pneumococcus	CSF result – gram positive pneumococcus
Rx IV benzyl penicillin 2gs 2 hly	Treatment with intravenous benzyl penicillin 2 grams given 2 hourly

ITU	Transfer to intensive care
Obs 15/60	Observations (pulse temperature respiration and blood pressure every 15 minutes)
neuro obs	Neuro obs as above

Orthopaedics

Orthopaedics

1. Anatomy and Physiology

Basic Terms

- Bones:
  Toughest tissue in body – either compact (appears solid to naked eye)
  Or cancellous (appearance like sponge).
- Muscles:
  Specialised tissue which has the ability to contract. When it contracts it causes movement.
- Nerves:
  Fibres which connect between organs and convey movement and sensation.
- Joints:
  Point of contact between two or more bones. Type of tissue varies according to joint and placement.
- Tendons:
  Cord of fibrous tissue which connects a muscle with some other structure.
- Ligaments:
  Fibrous tissue connecting bones together at the joints which allows for some movement.
- Cartilage
  Similar to gristle. Substance which is elastic and softer than bone. Its role is to provide structural support.

Types of Joints

- A. Fibrous/Fixed
  Immovable joint
- B. Cartilaginous/Slightly movable
  Between the vertebrae and slightly moveable
- C. Synovial/Freely movable
  Classified according to movement possible or to shape.

Types of synovial joint:

1. Ball and socket – (shoulder/hip)
   Wide range of movement

2. Gliding (between carpal and tarsal bones /hands and feet)
   Surfaces glide over each other

3. Pivot (radioulnar joint/wrist)
   Movement round one axis.

4. Hinge (elbow/knee)
   Allow flexion and extension only

The skeleton

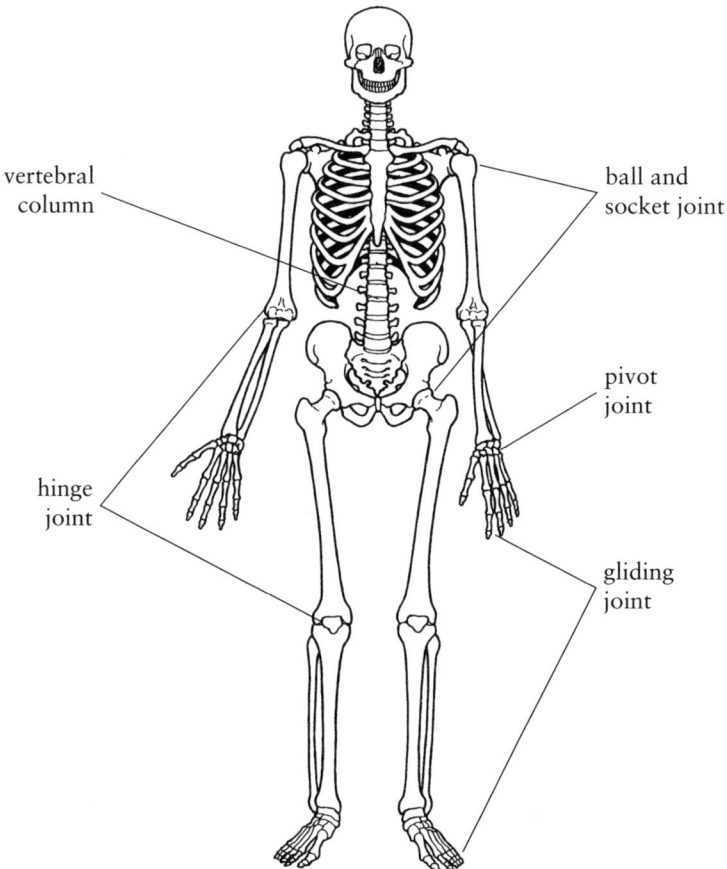

The Bones of the Head

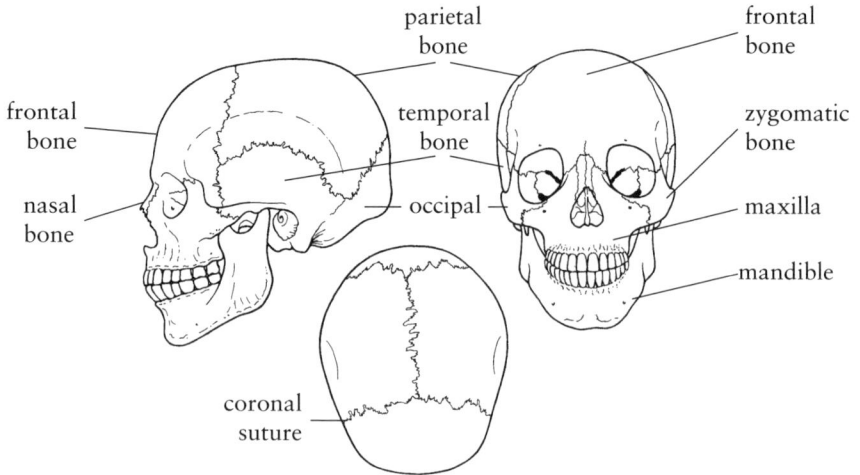

Vertebral Column

The vertebral column runs from the neck through to the rectum. There are thirty-three bones within the column some of which are fused and some of these are movable.

From the top of the neck downwards:

- Seven cervical vertebrae – moveable
- Twelve thoracic vertebrae – moveable
- Five lumbar vertebrae – moveable
- Five sacral vertebrae – fused
- Four coccyx vertebrae – fused

Vertebrae

Sacrum

These are five vertebrae, which are fused together. There are a series of holes in each bone (known as foramina) on either side, which allow for the passage of the nerves.

Coccyx

This is made of four fused vertebrae, which reduce in size until they reach a point at the end.

Functions of the vertebrae

The spinal cord runs through the middle and is protected from injury and trauma by the bony surrounds.

It allows for movement because of the number of bones.

It allows for the nerves and vessels to pass through to the different sections of the body.

It is sufficiently strong to support the skull, which is relatively heavy.

The discs placed between the vertebrae act as shock absorbers.

2. Symptoms

The major symptoms of orthopaedic disorders are:

A. Pain
B. Loss of movement
C. Swelling
D. Abnormal movement
E. Tenderness

3. Examination and Inspection

Examination follows the same principles as with any other area of medicine with a different approach when examination of the patient is required.

History

- Current complaint and symptoms
- Past medical history of note
- Past family history if relevant
- Social History/circumstances if relevant e.g. occupation/ problems with mobility/suitability of residence etc.

Examination

- Inspection – checking for deformity or differences in length, swelling etc.
- Palpation of the area (feeling gently for deformity, abnormality)
- Movement (checking whether the area is mobile and whether this is abnormal)
- Testing or straining the area (moving the part of the body to see if there is abnormal movement)

Examination: Orthopaedic Movements

- Abduction   – moving limb away from midline of body
                       – moving finger/toe from midline of foot
- Adduction   – moves towards the midline of the body
                       and may cross that line
- Circumduction   – moving arms or legs in circular
                       movement
- Eversion   – foot turned up and outwards
- Extension   – straightening out/bending backwards
- Flexion   – bending usually forward
- Inversion   – foot turned in and downwards
- Lateral flexion   – leaning head to side
- Lateral rotation   – rotating head so looking over shoulder
- Opposition   – thumb and little finger brought together

- Pronation   – hand turned downwards using forearm
                     – i.e. palm down
- Rotation   – movement along the long axis of a limb
- Supination   – hand turned upwards using forearm
                     – i.e. palm up

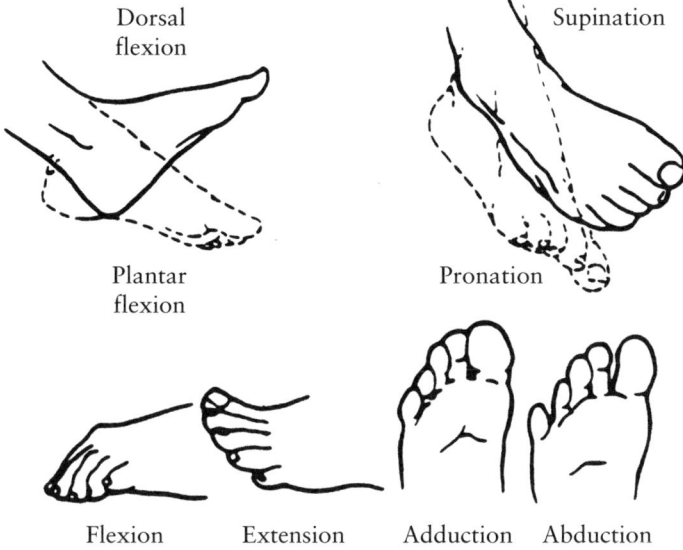

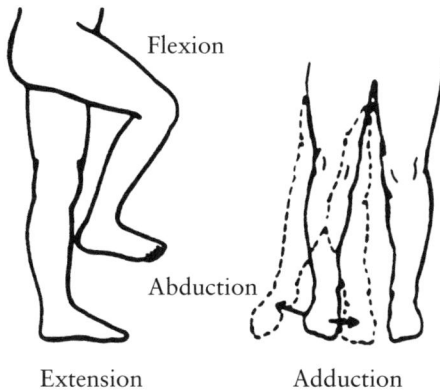

Dorsal flexion

Supination

Plantar flexion

Pronation

Flexion   Extension   Adduction   Abduction

Flexion

Abduction

Extension   Adduction

Outward rotation

Inward rotation

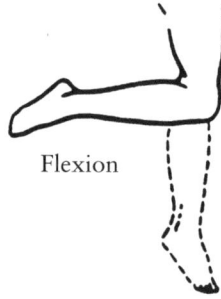

Flexion

Extension

Supination   Pronation

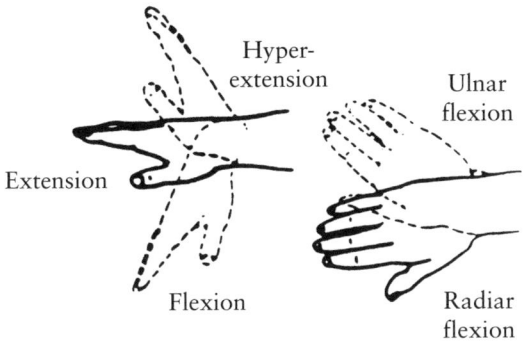

Hyper-extension

Ulnar flexion

Extension

Flexion

Radiar flexion

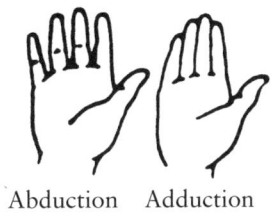

Abduction   Adduction

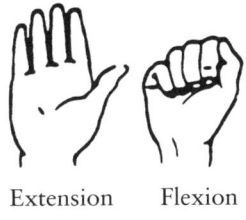

Extension   Flexion

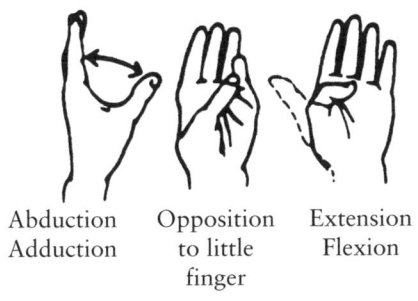

Abduction   Opposition   Extension
Adduction   to little   Flexion
             finger

Flexion   Extension   Hyper-
                          extension

Rotation   Lateral
                  flexion

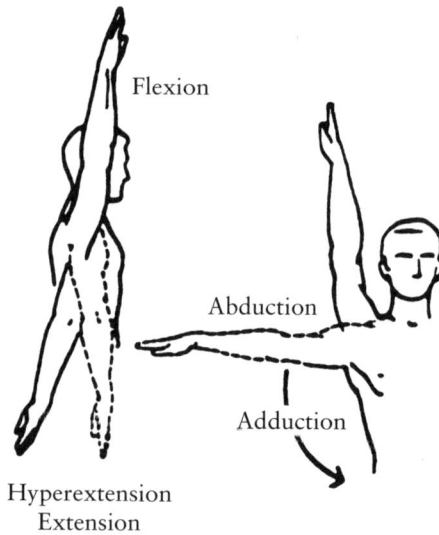

Flexion

Abduction

Adduction

Hyperextension
Extension

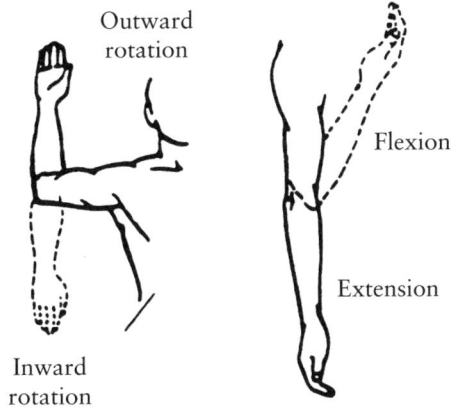

Outward rotation

Inward rotation

Flexion

Extension

Examination – Problems with Orthopaedic Structures

Muscles

Stressing or Straining –

Checking for weakness in muscle power
The effectiveness of how the muscle works is categorised by grades. O means no power, while 5 indicates full and normal power.

Grades of Muscle power
Grade 0	No Power in the muscle
Grade 1	Slight movement only
Grade 2	Only sufficient power to move a limb with gravity eliminated
Grade 3	Can move limb against gravity
Grade 4	Can move against active resistance. Sometimes categorised as + and ++
Grade 5	Full and normal power.

Ligaments

Weakness in ligaments
It is not possible to assess ligaments in the same way as muscles. They are assessed by checking whether there is an excessive or unusual movements.

Major Conditions

Traumas

a. Injuries to BONES
b   Injuries to JOINTS
c. Injuries to LIGAMENTS
d. Injuries to NERVES
e. Injuries to MUSCLES
f. Injuries to SKIN
g. Injuries to BLOOD VESSELS

A. Injuries to Bones and Joints

Fractures – usually abbreviated as #

Signs and Symptoms

- Abnormal movement
  (see orthopedic movements)
- Swelling
- Deformity, which can be seen or in some cases felt beneath the surface
- Tenderness
- Pain on movement
- Impaired function
- Grating between ends of bone (can be seen or usually felt)
- Bleeding/haemorrhage

Investigations

1. Patient History of events

2. Clinical examination

3. Abnormal movement, swelling, deformity, tenderness, pain, impaired function or grating.

4. X-rays – should usually be two planes (two views)
    Depends on site of fracture as to which x-rays are of more benefit – always check whether correct view has been taken.

5. Stress radiographs – examination of joints which have been loaded to locate any instability.

6. Scans

7. Arthroscopy (examination of the joints by camera)

8. Specific laboratory tests such as rheumatoid factor: these are general tests some of which may demonstrate a fracture

9. All tests for theatre – many fractures and major orthopaedic injuries require surgical intervention
Tests to be completed – full blood count, urea's & electrolytes, haemoglobin, chest x-ray

Complications

a. Bleeding
Bleeding – can be significant where major bones involved

b. Nerve damage

c. Damages to blood vessels

d. Damages to surrounding tissues

e. Infection
Particularly in open wound

f. Clotting problems
Can occur after a trauma but associated with significant blood loss

g Deformity
Usually occurs at a later stage

h. Osteoarthritis
Inflammation of the joint – usually where the uneven edges of the bones rub against each other. Can cause OA in bones further from site of fracture if effect is to place abnormal pressure on them.

i. Necrosis (death of tissue)
Also known as avascular necrosis
Usually major trauma where blood supply interrupted or stopped completely so underlying tissue dies. Bone will die without blood supply.

Areas of Fractures and Dislocations

Although all fractures will tend to have some similar symptoms and complications depending on the area affected there may be other issues which require consideration. The following is a basic review of the types of additional signs, investigations and issues which may be present when a particular area of the skeleton is affected. The medical records should therefore be checked to ensure that these additional points have been considered by medical staff.

1. **Cervical spine**

    History of events: Often occur in sport or road traffic accident. Fall on head with neck bent.

    Signs – may be unconscious. If head injury present or unconscious treat as for cervical spine injury
    Other signs – pain – which may radiate down arm, spasms of muscles and tenderness at neck.

    Investigations
    1. Inspection – log roll patient
    2. Neurological examination – check whether spinal cord damage, pin prick sensation including cranial nerves
    3. Radiology
       Spinal radiographs should usually include –
       anterior posterior (AP) (front to back),
       lateral (side) and if necessary – should show down to at least 7th vertebrae
       oblique (at angle –often 30 degrees).
       CT scans may provide clearer view
       MRI scan would normally demonstrate – cord compression or damage
    4. Theatre preparation if necessary

    Issues: Damage above level of C4 – will prevent respiratory muscles working.
    Treatment depends on type of fracture and whether it is stable.
    N.B.: Fractures of the C7 are often missed

2. **Thoracic spine:**
   History of events Usually fall from height/weight falling on back

   Signs: Local pain, bruising or marks over shoulders

   Investigations:
   1. Inspection of patient – log roll to inspect spine check for paraplegia
   2. Neurology – paraplegia common with dislocations
   3. Radiology – AP and lateral radiographs

3. **Lumbar spine**
   History of events: Usually – fall from height onto heels.

   Signs: pain over area and adjacent muscles

   Investigations:
   1. Inspection – Check for hip injury
   2. Neurological review – possibility of paraplegia if displacement of bone – possibility of cord damage
   3. Anterior-posterior and lateral x-rays

4. **Pelvic Fracture:**
   History of events: Common circumstances – the elderly following a fall or RTA

   Signs:
   - Pain and shock
   - Inability to pass urine
   - Bleeding from either urinary tract /rectum or vaginally
   - Examination of male rectum demonstrates the prostate in a high and unusual position

   Investigations:
   1. Inspection
   2. Neurological review – check for possibility of sciatic nerve damage
   3. Investigations – radiograph – pelvic x-ray CT scans/Urethrogram and IVU NB: undisplaced fracture of the pelvis are often missed

Issues: Number of other complications which need to be monitored:
- Haemorrhage and shock
- Damage to the bladder, urethra or rectum
- Could be damage to hip
- The gastrointestinal tract can stop working – (paralytic ileus)
- Can also develop blood clots in the legs (deep vein thrombosis)

5. Hip injuries

History of events: Usual – where RTA occurs and knee hits dashboard while hip is flexed

Signs:
- Real or apparent shortening compared to other non affected limb.
- Abnormal movement
- Pain in area and radiating down leg

Investigations
1. Inspection – check knee and leg for additional injury
2. Neurological review – common sciatic nerve damage in leg
3. Radiograph of hip, leg (femur) and knee
4. Theatre preparation

Issues: Posterior dislocations which are the most common have high incidence of complications including:
- Sciatic nerve damage
- Necrosis of the femoral head (death of the top end of femur)
- Osteoarthritis
- Ectopic Ossification – development of additional bone around the site
- Rupture of posterior cruciate ligament

6. Top of the femur (proximal femur fracture)

History of events: Elderly person with trip

Signs:
- Pain in area
- Shortening of limb
- Abnormal position of limb – externally rotated
- Abnormal movements of limb
- Unable to bear weight

Types of fracture: two types of fracture variously described but essentially are intracapsular or extracapsular.
- Intracapsular fractures are those which take place inside the capsule as below:
- Extracapsular fractures are those which take place outside the capsule as below:

The importance of the distinction is that the intracapsular fractures are more likely to lead to serious complications.

Investigations:
1. Inspection
2. Radiographs – two planes, possibly chest x-ray
3. Other tests – blood tests – Hb Haemoglobin for anaemia Full blood count, Urea and Electrolytes, blood sugar (where elderly concerned may be some underlying condition which requires treatment)
4. theatre preparation

Issues: Intracapsular fracture increases risk of:
a. Asceptic necrosis (can cut off the blood supply to the head of the femur completely)
b. Damage to the head of the femur through an increase in pressure due to trapped blood
c. Increased mobility inside the capsule because of the position of the fracture site. Difficult to address surgically
d. Increased pre-disposition to non union
e. Increased incidence of mal union and shortening of limb

Extracapsular fractures still run risk of above but less so.

7. **Fracture of the shaft of the Femur:**
   History of events: Commonly young people/RTA

   Signs:
   - Extreme pain in area
   - Deformed limb
   - Bleeding or nerve damage
   - Shock
   - Shortening of limb and abnormal positioning
   - Appears swollen due to muscle contraction

Investigations:
1. Inspection
2. Radiographs – two planes
3. Angiography if vascular injury is a possibility
4. Theatre preparation

Issues: Infection should be considered particularly if wound dirty
- Haemorrhage – substantial risk.
- Non union – requiring bone grafts
- Mal union
- Arterial damage – uncommon
- Nerve damage – uncommon but should be considered
- Shortening of limb

8. **Knee Fractures and dislocations:**
History of events: RTA or direct force. Dislocation can be recurrent – common in younger girls

Signs:
- Pain in area
- Swelling
- Tenderness on the site

Investigations:
1. Inspection
2. Radiographs – often demonstrate a haemarthrosis (blood in the joint cavity)
3. Stress radiographs may help
4. Arthroscopy
5. Theatre preparation

Issues:
- In comminuted fractures – rare for the knee (patella) to be saved. Often best to remove patella.
- Other fractures require immobilisation followed by physiotherapy
- Large fragments of bone can be fixed in place.
- Small fragments should be removed
- Osteoarthritis is a long term complication
- Recurrent dislocations may require surgery

9. **Tibial and fibulal fractures**
   History of events:
   - Tibia – RTA and sport
   - Fibula – rare on own – direct violence

   Signs:
   - Pain
   - Swelling
   - Deformity
   - Bleeding
   - Bruising
   - Unable to weight bear if tibia affected

   Investigations:
   1. Inspection
   2. Neurological – (common peroneal nerve can be affected by fibula fracture)
   3. Radiographs
   4. Theatre preparation

   Issues: Usual complications plus:
   - Risk of compartment syndrome (closed fracture where skin not broken causes blood and swelling internally. The space is closed and there is therefore pressure within the restricted space which cuts off blood supply to the area). The tissues can then die (necrosis).

10. **Fractures of the ankle**
    History of events: Usually indirect force or violence

    Signs:
    - Usual signs and symptoms of fractures
    - Often unable to weight bear

    Investigations:
    1. Inspection
    2. Neurological
    3. Radiographs lateral and AP
    4. Stress radiographs
    5. Possible preparation for theatre
    6. If rotation injury – ensure fibula checked for possible fracture of shaft

Issues
- Usual complications – effect can be more problematic because of reliance of feet
- Ligaments likely to be affected

11. Fractures of the feet and toes
History of events: Twisting injury or fall from height

Signs – as usual

Investigations – as usual

Issues –
- Fracture of the talus can lead to impairment of blood supply and avascular necrosis – rare fracture
- Fracture of the calcaneum can be difficult to detect on x-ray. check pattern of bruising and re check x-rays

12. Shoulder fractures and dislocations
History of events: Clavicular fracture/dislocation – fall on outstretched hand

Signs:
- Pain
- Shoulder droops due to weight of arm
- Dislocation – lack of feeling/anaesthesia

Investigations – usual
- Dislocation – check for associated fracture of humerus
- Nerve damage – fracture – brachial plexus. Dislocation axillary nerve
- Preparation for theatre

13. Fractures of the arm/Humerus injuries
History of events: Usually direct force – fracture of the shaft – direct blow or fall on outstretched hand.

Signs – as above.

Investigations – as above.

Issues: – possibility of radial nerve damage – where shaft affected.

Check for axillary nerve damage and axillary blood vessel damage where upper end of arm fractured

14. Fractures and dislocations of and at the elbow
Types of injury:
- Supracondylar – above the elbow joint
- Medial epicondyle –
- Lateral epicondyle injury
- Fractures
- Disclocations

History of events:
- Supracondular – child with outstretched arm
- Medial epicondyle and lateral epicondyle – children twisting or with force
- Fracture – direct force
- Dislocation – any age fall with outstretched hand

Signs – As above

Investigations – as above

Issues: Usual possible complications of orthopaedic trauma and surgery
In addition:
- *Supracondylar* fractures very difficult to treat
  Common vascular (blood supply) problems
  Compartment syndrome
  Volkmann's ishcaemic contracture – where muscle dies because of lack of blood supply, fibrous tissue takes its place and pulls fingers and wrist into flexion (droop)
  Nerve damage – median nerve
  Myositis ossificans – bony mass forms around muscles of elbow
- *Medial epicondyle* – as above
  Nerve damage – ulnar nerve
- *Fracture* – as above
  If significant disintegration of elbow – reassemble bones and fix internally
  Not good prognosis
- *Dislocation* – as above
  Stiffness
  Ectopic ossification – bony growth round soft tissue

15. Fracture of the wrist and lower arm

Common type – Colles

Within 1 inch of wrist, displaced backwards with the palm of the hand turned upwards

Others include – fracture of the radial head (wrist), radial and ulnar shafts (lower arm)

History of events:
- Colles elderly osteoporotic women. Young people sporting or active injury
- Others – direct violence

Signs as above

Colles – dinner fork appearance

Investigations as above

Issues – compartment syndrome can arise in wrist injuries. Colles fracture – sudek's atrophy (stiffness and lack of blood supply to hand – requires physiotherapy and is difficult to treat)

Nerve damage – median nerve

16. Scaphoid fractures

History of events: Fall on outstretched hand. Blow to palm of hand

Signs as above
- Tenderness in anatomical snuff box
- Swollen wrist i.e. just above the thumb

Investigations: As above. Scaphoid views on x-ray

Issues:
- Often difficult to detect on x-ray – treat as scaphoid and re-x-ray two weeks later to check
- Osteoarthritis
- Avascular necrosis (death of tissues due to inadequate blood supply) possible.

Terminology

Closed: Skin not broken. No evidence of soft tissue damage

Comminuted: Splinters off the bone. Difficult to move back into the correct position

Complicated: Usually indicates involvement of something else – nerves or blood supply for example

Crush: Often so severe that bone grafts are required to replace what left of the fractured bone.

Displaced: i.e. the bones sites have moved and are not directly in line with each other.

Greenstick: Children's fractures – Bones bend and split.

Impacted: Where end of one section of bone runs into the end of the other bone

Oblique fracture: Sometimes known as spiral. Often involves twisting motion. Fracture not clear across and more difficult to move into the correct shape.

Open fracture: Skin broken and soft tissue damage in addition to type of fracture

Pathological: Weakened bones due to osteoporosis/cancer etc.

Segmental: Free floating section of bone not attached at either end. Difficult to mend without some form of fixation device (usually internal)

Stable: Able to keep in position to allow for mending

Transverse fracture: Cut through the bone. Usually able to move back into shape relatively easily

Undisplaced: Bone ends are in correct position despite fracture

Unstable: Liable to move

B. Injuries to Joints

Injuries to joints are essentially dislocations. These tend to be graded according to their severity:–

- A **Subluxation** is a partial dislocation. These often do not require any active treatment aside from painkillers and rest.
- A **Dislocation** requires active treatment. Usually this involves replacing the joint in to its appropriate place. Sometimes joints, which have been dislocated, have an increased propensity to suffer the same problems again.
- A **Fracture Dislocation** is the most severe form because it is complicated by a fracture in addition to the dislocation. It often requires surgical intervention to fix the bones into the appropriate place.

C. Injuries to Ligaments

Types of injuries

a. Sprain/Strain

The ligament is torn slightly and there will be bruising at the site with pain often for several weeks or more. However the joint is stable and treatment of the symptoms is all that is usually required.

b. Partial Tear

This is where the tear is more significant although not necessarily larger. The joint is no longer stable and a plaster cast is usually required to maintain stability and protect the area while the ligament heals

c. Rupture/Complete Tear

A complete rupture, similar to a fracture dislocation will usually require surgical intervention. Conservative treatment can be often effective.

Signs of ligamentous damage

a. Pain at site
b. Tenderness
c. Bruising
d. Swelling

e. Abnormal movement
f. Muscle spasm
g. Pain on use
h. Most useful is HISTORY OF EVENTS

Investigation

- Inspection
- Radiographs are of little use but may eliminate fractures
- Arthroscopy
- Preparation for theatre where surgery required

Common sites of ligament damage

Knee
The knee has a number of ligaments on which it relies for stability:–

(a) Anterior Cruciate ligament
- Usually sharp twisting movement
- Signs as above plus: patient sometimes hears sharp breaking sound
- Unstable movement – difficult to assess instability after short period because of muscle spasm

(b) Posterior Cruciate Ligament
- Usually force to upper end of tibia when sitting on motorbike or in car
- Signs: as above plus backward droop of tibia
  Haemarthrosis (blood in tissues causing swelling)

Ankle
- Sprained ankle – partial tear of anterior inferior talofibular ligament
- Lateral collaterol ligament rupture
- Signs as above
- Investigations as usual but stress radiographs are sometimes helpful

D. Injuries to Nerves

Neuropraxia

Transient loss of function. Usually recovers spontaneously.

Axonotmesis

Longer loss of function. Usually takes several weeks or months to recover.

Neurotmesis

Where the nerve has actually been severed. Recovery will not be possible without surgical intervention. Results of operations vary according to site and length of time which has elapsed prior to surgery.

Signs and symptoms
- Pain – can be referred to another area
- Paraesthesia – lack of feeling in affected area
- Weakness in the affected area

Investigations
- Neurological studies
- Nerve Conduction Studies – stimulation of the nerve with a pulse and measuring its flow to a pre arranged point.
- Electromyogram (muscle studies)
- Reflexes – simple form of nerve behaviour. Stimulus produces instant response along nerve pathway.

Susceptible areas
- Sciatic nerve – affects legs – hip and spinal damage
- Common peroneal nerve – affects knee and lower leg – top of fibula damaged
- Ulnar nerve – affects little finger and ring finger –
- Radial nerve – affects palm and wrist – damage to upper arm and elbow
- Brachial plexus – affects lower arm and wrist – develops droop – damage to shoulder and cervical spine
- Cervical nerve roots – widespread problems depending on severity and site – upper limbs – damage to neck

- Lumbar nerve roots – widespread problems depending on severity and site – lower limbs – damage to lower back

Carpal tunnel syndrome – median nerve damage

Compression of the median nerve leading to muscle wastage and loss of feeling in the hand.

Signs
- Paraesthesia in fingers (not little finger or palm) – worse at night
- Tingling or pain in same area
- Muscle wastage

Investigations
- Inspection
- Tinel's sign – tap on median nerve at wrist and if exacerbated – positive sign
- Electromyographic studies
- Nerve conduction studies

Issues
- Common in pregnancy where fluid retained and swelling occurs
- Common in general practice
- Patient who comments all fingers affected – requires investigation but should be treated with suspicion.

E. Injuries to Muscles and Tendons

Muscles and tendons can suffer a number of injuries depending on the nature of the trauma.

Muscles can be injured in the following ways:

a. They can be **severed.** Repairs are often unsuccessful
   Some force can crush them.

b. A reduction in blood supply (**Ischaemia**) can affect function and lead to necrosis (death)

c. They can also suffer from excess and misplaced bone fragments which develop from fracture sites. This is known as **Ossification.**

d. a blood clot can be found within the muscle **Haematoma.**

e. The muscle or the tendon can be **Ruptured.**
Muscles are often damaged with tendons.

Signs of muscular and tendon damage

a. tearing sensation
b. swelling and tenderness
c. bruising
d. with repetitive use the tendons can become inflamed and pain can be caused at the site of the injury and on use.

Investigations

1. Inspection and history of incident/condition
2. Radiographs to exclude arthritis or other condition
3. Ultrasound – also used for treatment in some cases
4. Electromyogram (EMG) detects the electrical activity in muscles

Issues

- Haematoma – can be serious problem because it can ossify leading to bone formation in incorrect place
- Surgery often unsuccessful
- Avoidance of contraction of the muscle necessary following acute injury
- Ice, compression and elevation recommended where soft tissue damage
- Local injections of steroids where area affected is the tendon attachment to the bone.

F. Injuries to Skin

The most usual injury to skin is that of **laceration.** Depending on size, site and bleeding most can be repaired either naturally or via surgery.

In some cases injury takes place which peels off the skin (for example when a limb becomes trapped). This is known as **degloving**. Depending on the size and site a skin graft may be needed to deal with the problem.

G. Injuries to Blood Vessels

These can be **lacerated** or **crushed**. A simple division of a vessel may be repairable by surgery or cauterisation. A more complex or significant crush may require resection (removal) of the part. Where an artery or major vein in concerned the consequences of failing to act quickly may be fatal. Where a minor vessel is concerned repair may take place without the need for surgery or even medical attention.

Other Common Conditions

Osteoarthritis

This is the gradual breakdown between the surfaces of joints. It can result from trauma. Inflammation occurs.

Usually it happens in large joints. There are several stages of deterioration.

Signs
- Pain,
- Loss or alteration of movement
- Deformity

Investigations
- Inspection – reduced range of movement, swelling of joints
- Radiographs – narrowing of joint space apparent – development of osteophytes – unusual bony growth
- Blood tests to exclude other causes of condition

Treatment
- Drugs – anti inflammatory (non steroid usually) – Injections of steroids
- Physiotherapy/hydrotherapy
- Surgery – variety available including but not limited to replacement

Reumatoid arthritis

- Inflammation of the joints.
- Can be the result of deficiencies in immune system – not local trauma
- Has acute and chronic phases.
- Usually smaller joints – hands and feet

Signs

- Pain
- Increased temperature (pyrexia) when acute phase of condition
- Deformity
- Swelling

Investigations

- Inspection – particularly tender and swollen joints, hot and painful to move
- Radiographs
- Full Blood Count – ESR – raised as a result of abnormal autoimmune system
- Serum uric acid – to exclude gout
- Rheumatoid factor – positive in 80% cases
- Antinuclear antibody test – should be negative to exclude SLE (systemic lupus erythematosus)

Treatment

- Drugs – including anti inflammatory (non steroidal/steroids/ gold/metholrexate (and many others))
- Rest when acute stage. Mobility when remission
- Surgery – different types pf surgery available for RA and OA (rheumatoid and osteo arthritis).

Osteomyelitis

- Infection of the bone
- Can be acute or chronic.
- Infection in bone often after minor trauma

Signs

- Usual signs of infection
- High temperature (pyrexia)
- Pain (extremely painful)

- Localized tenderness
- Development of pus
- Destruction of the bone

Investigations
- Full blood count – White cell count should be elevated
                        Increase in ESR
- Blood cultures
- Radiographs – little assistance in early stage
- Bone scan
- CT scan

Treatment
- Antibiotics – often for very long periods
- Surgery – remove dead bone/clean out of pus/infected tissue

Osteoporosis

- Reduction in bone tissue. Inability of body to keep pace with amount needed.
- Can be local in effect or can be widespread.
- Result of reduction of collagen in bones of post menopausal women, weaker bones prone to fracture
- Can be diffuse (widespread) where confined to bed after major illness or trauma
- Steroid therapy can cause.

Signs
- Tendency to fracture
- Pain
- Thinner bones on x-ray

Investigations
- Inspection – rarely of use
- History of importance for example, a number of fractures in recent years
- Bone densitometry (review of density of bones) – once diagnosis possible
- Radiographs show loss of bone density when 30–50% reduction in bone mass

Treatment
- Depends on cause –
- Can be hormone replacement therapy/reduction in steroids
- Mobilisation

Principles of Treatment

1. Traction/Immobilisation

Traction is the process whereby weights pull bones into alignment. It can be applied by:

a. **Skeletal** traction – using pins through the bones
b. **Skin** traction – adhesive strapping to skin

Other forms of immobilisation of limbs:

a. Slings
b. Splints which can be made of plaster of Paris or any other reasonably rigid material.

2. Surgery

Common operations

• Replacements:	Total hip replacement (THR)
	Total Knee replacement (TKR)
• Arthroplasty	joint replacement
• Pin and plating	securing joint
• Meniscectomy	removal of the meniscus
• Examination under anaesthetic (EUA)	
• Manipulation under anaesthetic (MUA)	
• Reductions	Reducing fractures so stable (placing in good position)
• Laminectomy	removal of part of disc (spinal)
• Discectomy	removal of disc

Common terms and abbreviations

Terms

ARTHRODESIS	fusion of a joint
ARTHROTOMY	opened joint
ARTHROPLASTY	refashioned or replacement of a joint
ARTHROLYSIS	mobilised
SYNOVECTOMY	excision of the synovium
OSTEOTOMY	cut into bone
OSTEOSYTHESIS	joined bone
EXOSTECTOMY	smoothed bone
NEUROPRAXIA	transient loss of function to nerves
AXONOTMESIS	loss of function due to severe compression
NEUROTEMESIS	division of the nerve. No recovery unless Repaired

Abbreviations

THR	total hip replacement
TKR	total knee replacement
CDH	congenital dislocated hip
OA	osteo arthritis
RA	rheumatoid arthritis
PA	protrusio acetabuli
AS	Ankylosing spondylitis
ORIF	Open reduction and internal fixation (very common operation for fractures)

Clinical records

Ambulance A & E	Came via ambulance into Accident and emergency department
63 yr woman H$_x$ O recent fall	63 year old woman with history of recent fall
C/o pain in L hip radiating down leg	Complaining of pain in left hip which radiates down leg
↓ mobility	Decrease in mobility
PMHX THR 1994 ®	Past medical history – total hip replacement in 1994 – right hip
Δ osteoporosis 1996 - Ca supplements HRT	Diagnosed with osteoporosis in 1996 receiving calcium supplements and hormone replacement therapy
?CVA 1999 - ?TIA	Possible stroke in 1999, possible transient ischaemic attack
° medication	No medication
Nil else	Nothing else of significance
FHX Widow - H RIP 1996 O children	Family history, Husband died in 1996 no children
O/E L hip - rotated external	On examination – left hip is rotated externally
Shortened swelling ° bleeding apparent	Is shorter limb than right Swelling present but no signs of bleeding

Neuro - NAD	Neurological examination – nothing abnormal detected
For PXR hip, femur	For pelvic, hip and leg x-rays
FBC, ECG U & Es	Full blood count, electrocardiogram and urea and electrolytes
?Δ # neck of femur	Possible diagnosis fractured neck of femur
Refer ortho	Refer to orthopaedic team
admit	Admit
XRY - Δ # neck of femur	X-ray confirms diagnosis
For theatre: mane	For theatre in morning

Gynaecology

Gynaecology

Anatomy and Physiology

The external aspects of the female reproductive system are well known and consist of:

Labia majora
Labia minora
Clitoris
Vestibule
Hymen
Greater vestibule glands

The Internal Organs of the female reproductive system are:

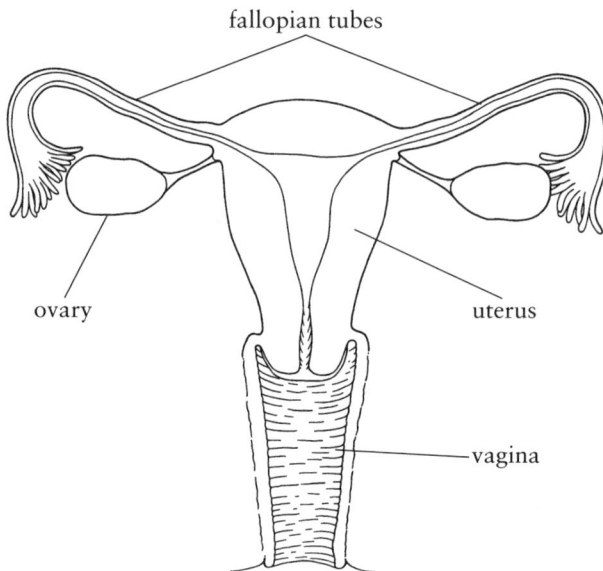

fallopian tubes

ovary

uterus

vagina

Vagina

The vagina has three layers of tissue. It has no secretory glands of its own but is kept moist by cervical secretions. On the whole the vagina is acidic. It is supplied by blood via the arterial plexus. There is lymph drainage and the nerve supply includes both parasympathetic and sympathetic nerve fibres.

Uterus

The uterus lies in the pelvic cavity between the bladder and the rectum. In most women it is anteflexed (bent forward) but in some women it is anteverted (leans forward). The uterus has a fundus (the top dome shaped section), a body being the main part and the os – either the internal os (next to the cervix) or the external os (where it was linked to the cervix).

The uterus has three layers of tissue:

The perimetrium

This includes all peritoneum and the broad ligament

The Myometrium

This is the thickest layer of tissue. It consists of smooth muscle fibres plus blood vessels and nerves.

The Endometrium

Consists of mucus secreting tubular glands. Upper third of cervical canal lined with mucous membrane. Lower third lined with alternative type of epithelium similar to that of the vagina.

The uterine arteries and veins supply the uterus. There are also a variety of lymph glands and a nerve supply.

The uterus is supported in the pelvic cavity by two broad ligaments. They hand down from the uterine tubes and are enclosed in the upper free border and near this lateral ends they penetrate the posterior wall. In between the broad ligaments are other sections of ligaments. There are round ligaments, uterosacral ligaments and transverse cervical ligaments, which also support the uterus and surrounding structures.

Fallopian Tubes

These are approximately 10 centimetres long and connect the uterus to the area of the ovaries. At the end of each tube there are finger like projections, which are called fimbriae. The role of the fallopian tubes is to convey the ovum to the uterus by movement. Fertilisation occurs in the fallopian tubes.

Ovaries

Ovaries are the female equivalent of the gonads. They are attached to the uterus by the mesovarium and the ligament of the ovary. Within the mesovarium the blood vessels and nerves travel.

The ovaries consist of two layers of tissue: the medulla, which includes the blood vessels and nerves and the cortex, which includes the follicles. Each follicle contains an ovum (egg). These are released on a monthly basis during childbearing or reproductive years.

Hormonal issues

The anterior pituitary gland, which is situated in the brain, stimulates the two main hormones, which affect the reproductive system for women. The anterior pituitary stimulates the release of **Follicle Stimulating Hormone** (FSH), which stimulates the follicles. While maturing the lining cells of the follicle release **Oestrogen**. After ovulation the anterior pituitary releases **Luteinising Hormone** (LH) which influences the lining cells to develop into the corpus luteum (Yellow body). The corpus luteum in turn produces progesterone.

If the ovum is not fertilised the corpus luteum degenerates and menstruation occurs. If the ovum is fertilised it will embed into the wall of the uterus. As it grows and develops it produces **Human Chorionic Gonadotrophin** (HCG), which in turn will stimulate the corpus luteum to continue producing progesterone.

Gynaecological Records

1. Referral letter from GP

2. Brief review of history of complaint and reason for referral from GP with details of any tests and investigations completed (e.g. smear test result)

3. Clinical records – clerking, outpatient and admission notes

4. Clerking notes – taken on admission if emergency or in outpatient department if referred to clinic.

5. Operative records if appropriate

6. Results and reports

7. Nursing kardex and careplan

Clerking notes should include:

- Current complaint
- Past medical history
- Social history
- Family history
- History of current complaint
- On examination findings
- Investigations and tests required
- Possible diagnosis
- Treatment plan

Gynaecological Clerking

1. *History from Patient*

Should include:

a. **Menstrual cycle**
- Date of commencement of menstruation – *menarche*
- Menstrual Cycle – length, timing, regularity, heaviness, painfulness
- Last menstrual period
- Intermittent bleeding

N.B. Common terms for menstrual irregularities covering timings and frequencies include:–

No periods	amenorrhoea
Frequent	polymenorrhoea
Infrequent	oligomenorrhoea
Heavy regular	Menorrhagia
Heavy irregular	Metrorrhagia
Frequent and heavy	Polymenorrhagia

b. **Urinary symptoms**
   - Pain on passing urine (micturating)   Dysuria
   - Blood in urine   Haematuria
   - Going to toilet frequently   Frequency
   - Going to pass urine in the night   Nocturia

c. **Sexual History**
   - When started
   - How many partners (i.e. multiple, single etc)
     e.g: Pain on intercourse Dyspareunia
   - Infection history if applicable:
     E.g.: Syphilis
            Warts
            Herpes genitalis
            Gonorrhoea
            Pelvic inflammatory disease
            HIV and AIDS

d. **Obstetric history**
   - Previous pregnancies
   - How many successful
   - What age and sex
   - Problems with pregnancy
     (**See** Obstetric Clerking Records)

e. **Other signs and symptoms**
   - Pruritis (Itching of vagina)

f. **All other relevant medical history**
   including if necessary family history

2. Gynaecological Examination

This examination should include:

a. Breast examination – not always completed depends on the complaint/condition

b. abdominal examination

   - Appearance
   - Percussion – tapping the abdomen
   - Palpation (gently feeling the abdomen)

c. Pelvic examination

   - Lithotomy position – legs in stirrups
   - Examination of the external genitalia
   - Speculum insertion – to enable viewing of the cervix
   - If prolapse of vaginal wall possibility – may examine on side by using a Sims speculum
   - Vaginal examination – use of fingers

d. Possible rectal examination – where mass is suspected which may affect rectal area

3. Tests and Investigations

a. Pregnancy test –

   - if suspected or intermenstrual or post coital (after sex) bleeding

b. Smear –

   - if suspicion of infection or malignancy

c. Blood tests:

   - Haemoglobin – if heavy periods
   - FSH – follicle stimulating hormone – ? suspicion of menopause/ absence or reduction in periods
   - Testosterone – raised level could indicate polycystic ovarian disease (Multiple cysts of ovaries)

- Prolactin – hormone which develops and assists milk production

d. Other tests:

  - Thyroid tests   T4
  - EMU   Early morning urine specimen
  - HVS   High vaginal swab – Test for variety of infections
  - MSU   Mid stream urine specimen
  - Pap smear   Ordinary smear taken to test for cancerous changes in cells of cervix

e. Scans

  - Ultrasound – heavy periods or irregular bleeding
                Possibility of endometriosis
  - Hysterosalpingogram (HSG) – flow of contrast dye through the reproductive system
  - Radiology – to exclude pelvic problems
  - CT scan
  - Mammogram – scan of breasts

f. Scopes

  - Colposcopy – cervix and vagina
  - Laparoscopy – general scope into abdomen to review area
  - Hysteroscopy – scope via vagina into cervix and uterus

g. Biopsy

  - Cone biopsy – section of cervix removed either to remove malignant or suspicious cells or to review tissue to assist diagnosis

Diagnoses

a. Condition requiring review
b. Condition requiring medical treatment
c. Condition requiring surgery

a. Review

An example of a condition requiring review would be a slightly abnormal smear test which is not indicative of cancerous changes but needs a further test six months later.

Another example would be abnormality of menstruation which may require review in 6–12 months.

b. Medical treatment

Infections

Examples of conditions requiring medical treatment would be infections.

Not all of these are sexually transmitted but affect the genito urinary system.

Treatment regimes change but when reviewing records check for the following:

Infection	Investigations and signs	Treatments
Candida	Pruritis Dysuria (pain on passing urine) Dyspareunia (pain on intercourse) High vaginal swab	Clotrimazole pessaries (anti fungal) Information on hygiene Treat partner
Chlamydia	Can be asymptomatic Dysuria Offensive discharge with mucus Swab	Refer to GU clinic Tetracycline Can become chronic infection – causing infertility and pelvic inflammatory disease
Gardnerella	Fishy smelling discharge Discoloured discharge High Vaginal swab	Metronidazole (antibiotic)
Genital herpes	Clinical appearance Symptoms – Itching lesions Crusted ulcers Swab from lesion	Salt water baths and ice packs during acute stage Analgesia Acyclovir derivative – (anti viral)

Infection	Investigations and signs	Treatments
Genital warts	Clinical appearance Soft moist swellings grow rapidly Pap smear required before treatment	Refer GU clinic Local administration of Podophyllin to warts Cauterise or cryosurgical removal (essentially burn of freeze from position)
Gonorrhoea	Dysuria Frequency Vaginal discharge Smear	Refer to GU Also test for syphillis Amoxycillin
Syphillis	Primary lesion can form ulcer Secondary stage – rash Tertiary or late stage – lesion destroying surrounding tissue. Can affect cerebral function Virological studies Blood tests CSF examination Darkfield examination – skilled miscroscopy review	Penicillin drug of choice Rare to develop to tertiary stage Needs post treatment tests to ensure cleared
Trichomonas Vaginalis (known as TV)	Frothy and yellow discharge Dysuria Dyspareunia Surface of cervix may show strawberry spots on examination High vaginal swab Ordinary (pap) smear will detect	Metronidazole (antibiotic)

Also AIDs and HIV – the details of which are beyond this book

Other main conditions

The main conditions in gynaecology which are considered on clerking and review:

Condition	Signs	Investigations	Treatment options
Amenorrhoea *Absence of menstruation*	No periods	History Clinical examination Pregnancy test Blood hormone levels X-ray and ultrasound Weight Pituitary testing if suspicious of a mass	Varies according to cause
Bleeding (abnormal) *Irregular or heavy bleeding*	Bleeding irregularly in amount or time Bleeding in between periods	History Clinical examination Pap Smear High vaginal swab Full blood count Ultra sound and/or x-ray laparoscopy	Depends on cause Surgery is indicated if malignancy is cause
Endometriosis *Presence of endometrial tissue from uterus in abnormal locations*	Infertility Dysmenorrhoea Dysparuenia Can form cysts – ENDOMETRIOMAS containing blood – giving chocolate appearance. Known as chocolate cysts. Can rupture but are difficult to remove.	Ultra sound Laparoscopy	Danazol (Unpleasant side effects) Surgery

Condition	Signs	Investigations	Treatment options
Pelvic inflammatory disease *(pain and inflammation in pelvis)*	Pain	Description and history of pain Smear Swab – high vaginal and endocervical Blood tests (depending on circumstances) Ultrasound Laparoscopy	Antibiotics Information
Salpingitis *(inflammation due to infection of the fallopian tubes)*	Pain – severe lower abdominal pain guarding vomiting high fever discharge	History – insertion of IUCD (intra uterine contraceptive device), recent sex, childbirth or abortion Temperature and white cell count elevated On examination – moving cervix causes pain Culture and smear tests of discharge	Antibiotics Fluids Treatment of symptoms as necessary

Additional disorders

1. **Menstrual disorders:**

    Menstruation is discharge of blood on (usually) a 28–35 day cycle during the reproductive years.

    A. Dysmenorrhoea – primary or secondary

    - Primary: Pain immediately before and during the first few hours of menstruation.
    - Secondary: pain few days before and increasing. May last few days into period.

B. Amenorrhoea (See table)

- Absence of menstruation. – primary or secondary
- Primary: Late onset of menstruation: i.e. 16 years or older
- Secondary: Menstruation has occurred but ceases for a period of six months or more.

C. Menorrhagia

- Heavy menstrual loss.
  (80mls loss during period – normal 30 mls)

D. Dysfunctional uterine bleeding (DUB)

- Abnormal bleeding where organic cause can not be identified.
- Can include menorrhagia and haemorrhage. Can occur around time of menopause – need to check for malignancy

E. Pre menstrual Syndrome

- Collection of symtoms which occur immediately prior to commencement of period including pain, discomfort, changes in mood, breast tenderness.

2. **Sexual disorders**
   A. Apareunia

- Absence of intercourse: inability to have intercourse
- Can include impotence, absence of vagina, imperforate hymen

B. Dypareunia

- Painful intercourse
- Can be superficial/Deep:–
  Superficial: pain on penetration can be caused by infections/menopause
  Deep:Pain on deep penetration – usually organic cause including endometriosis and pelvic inflammatory disease

C. Impotence

D. Frigidity

3. **Infective disorders – see table for specific infections**
   A. Cervix

   - Cervicitis – (inflammation of cervix)
   - Purulent discharge, backache, pain, pain on passing urine and on sexual intercourse

   B. Vulva/vagina

   - Vulvovaginitis:
   - Itching and pain on intercourse.
   - Reddening of skin
   - Discharge and pain on passing urine

   C. Common sexual transmitted disease

   D. Fallopean tubes/salpingitis

4. **Endometrial Disorders**
   A. Endometriosis: – see table

   B. Adenomyosis:

   - Presence of endometrial tissue within uterine cavity but placed wrongly inside the myometrium (inner layer).
   - Pain during period – increasing and heavy blood flow (menorrhagia)

5. **Disorders of the Cervix**
   A. Benign: polyps

   - tumour arising out of mucous membranes
   - irregular bleeding. bright red appearance
   - rare to have malignant changes

   B. Benign: Fibroids:

   - connective tissue tumour. Usually uterine.
   - Pain – spasmodic at times of menstruation

C. Malignant: Cancer

- Detected by pap smear
- Pap (papanicolaou) Grouping for smears is as follows:

Group 1   Normal cells
Group 2   Normal cells with some normal variants
Group 3   Unusual cells present. Probably not malignant
Group 4   Individual cells present indicating malignancy
Group 5   Considerable numbers of atypical cells indicating malignancy

- Cancer Stages
Carcinoma is staged as a means of classification.
It is a means by which oncologists can communicate the development of the condition.

There are five stages in cancers – stage O–IV:–

Stage 0
cancer present in cervix

Stage I:
Ia   confined to cervix BUT has invaded tissue to 5mm
Ib   still confined to cervix BUT more than 5mm depth in tissues

Stage II
IIa   extends beyone cervix but has not reached pelvic wall has reached vagina but not lower third of the vagina. No obvious signs that it has reached connective tissue (parametrial tissue) surrounding uterus.
IIb   extends beyond cervix but hs not reached pelvic wall. Has reached vagina not lower third. Obvious signs that it has reached the parametrial tissue surrounding uterus.

Stage III
IIIa   has not yet reached lateral (side) pelvic wall but has reached lower third of vagina.
IIIb   has reached pelvic wall and problems with one kidney resulting

Stage IV
IVa Spread to adjacent organs
IVb Spread to distant organs and structures

Cancer Treatment:

Cancer treatments change over time but as a rough guide the following is common:

1. Cauterisation:
    Similar to a laser or diathermy (cells burnt out)

2. Surgery:
    Cone Biopsy
    Total abdominal hysterectomy –
    Radical hysterectomy and pelvic node dissection

3. Radiotherapy

6. Disorders of the ovaries
- Torsion (twisting)
- Rupture (splits and spills contents)
- Haemorrhage
- Hormone production – irregular menstrual cycle

7. Disorders of support
- Cystocoele   prolapse of vaginal wall affecting bladder
- Rectocoele   hernia of vagina through rectum
- Urethrocoele   prolapse vaginal wall affecting urethra
- Enterocoele   prolapse of Pouch of Douglas i.e. recto-uterine pouch

Surgery in Gynaecology

Common Surgical operations in Gynaecology

a. Hysterectomy

- TAH – Total Abdominal Hysterectomy
- Removal of uterus – often with BSO (bilateral salpingo oophrectomy) – removal of fallopian tubes and ovaries

- Wertheims – removal of uterus and 1/3 of cervix (usually completed for cancer)

b. Sterilisation
   Methods include:

   - Hulka clip – attached to the tube
   - Ligation of tube
   - Filschie clip

c. Myomectomy
   Removal of the inner lining (the myometrium) of the Uterus usually for fibroids
   Haemorrhage – significant risk

d. Vulvectomy
   Removal of all or part of the vulva – usually due to cancer

e. Oophrectomy
   Removal of the ovary or ovaries – usually due to cancer

f. Salpingectomy
   Removal of one or both of the fallopian tubes due to either cancer or an ectopic pregnancy (pregnancy which has developed outside of the womb)

g. Termination
   Termination of pregnancy. Different techniques depending on the age of the fetus

h. Cone Biopsy
   Removal of cone shaped section of the cervix usually because of cancerous cells.

i. Colporrhaphy
   Surgical treatment of a prolapse of the vaginal wall which affects the bladder.

Gynaecological Records

There are specific issues in records for gynaecological patients as follows

1. Pre operatively

a. thorough gynae history reviewed

b. investigations may include the additional:

- ultra sound scan,
- pap smear,
- high vaginal swab
- colposcopies and
- biopsies
- blood tests for LH and F S H levels (luteinising hormone and follicle stimulating hormone)

2. Peri operatively (during surgery)

Positions:

- Lithotomy
- Supine
- Prone (rare)
- Lateral (rare)

3. Post Operatively

Nursing kardex will record details of loss of blood or other fluids by vagina because of:–
Increased risks of:

- Haemorrhage
- Risk of infection
- Risk of urinary problems
- Risk of paralytic ileus (section of bowel stops working effectively)

Gynaecological cancer

	Cervix	Ovaries	Uterus	Vagina	Vulva
Stage 0	In cervix only	In ovaries only	In uterus only	In vagina only	In vulva only
Stage Ia	cervix only. Depth 5mm	One ovary. Tumour possibly on external surface. Capsule could be ruptured	Uterus only. Less than 8cm	Limited to vaginal walls	Confined to vulva. 2cms or less
Stage Ib	Cervix but more than 5mm	Limited to both ovaries. Capsule could be ruptured and tumour on external surface	Uterus but larger than 8 c.m.s	N/A	N/A
Stage Ic	N/A	Stage 1a or 1b with ascites	N/A	N/A	N/A
Stage IIa	Beyond cervix. Not to side pelvic wall. Vagina but not lower $^1/_3$. No obvious parametrial involvement	1 or more ovaries. Pelvic involvement. Extension to uterus and tubes	Uterus and cervix	Subvaginal tissue. No pelvic wall	More than 2 c.m.s in diameter. Nodes could be palpable and mobile
Stage IIb	As above with obvious parametrial involvement	As above with extension to other pelvic tissues	N/A	N/A	N/A
Stage IIc	N/A	As above with ascites/ malignant cells in peritoneal fluid	N/A	N/A	N/A
Stage IIIa	Not extended to side pelvic wall but involves lower $^1/_3$ vagina	One or both ovaries. secondaries in peritoneum. extension to bowel or omentum	Outside uterus but not pelvis	Extended to side pelvic wall	Spread to lower urethra +/or vagina, peritoneum/ anus AND/OR nodes in 1 or more groins, enlarged, firm and NOT fixed

	Cervix	Ovaries	Uterus	Vagina	Vulva
Stage IIIb	Pelvic wall and kidney involved	N/A	N/A	N/A	N/A
Stage IVa	Beyond pelvis. Adjacent organs	One or more ovaries. Distant secondaries	Adjacent organs. Beyond pelvis	Adjacent organs	Bladder or rectum involvement. Upper part of urethra

Stage 0	**Local only.**
Stage I	**Confined to area but local infiltration.**
Stage II	**Beyond organ/area. Limited within pelvis.**
Stage III	**Affecting other areas outside pelvis.**
Stage IV	**Spread outside to distant organs.**

N.B. Stages can change and be further sub divided over time.

Typical Records
of Gynaecological Patient

Records	Explanation:
35 yr elective admission	35 years old. Planned admission
C/o dysmenorrhoea	Complaining of painful periods
And Menorrhagia	Heavy periods
PMHX - G4 P3-1 Male 8, 2 Female 3,6	Past medical history 4 previous pregnancies, 3 successful. One male child aged 8, 2 girls aged 3 and 6
TOP 1990	Termination of pregnancy 1990
Abnormal smear? 1995	Abnormal smear? 1995
Colposcopy NAD	Colposcopy nothing abnormal detected
Pap 1999 - CIN 3	Smear recently – CIN3 (see cancer section)
ψ depression. Saw pysch	Psychiatric – history depression saw psychiatrist
On MAOIs	Types of anti depressants
Nil else of note	Nothing else of significance
FHX - married. H supportive	Family history married with supportive husband
Teacher	As indicated
O/E anxious	On examination – anxious

Records	Explanation:
Pain R LQ	Pain in the right lower quadrant (of the abdomen)
VE NAD	Vaginal examination – nothing abnormal detected
O masses	No masses felt
For USS	For Ultra sound scan
PXR	Pelvic x-ray
CXR	Chest x-ray
ECG	Electrocardiogram (for surgery)
FBC & X match	Full blood count and ensure type known and supplies available if needed
MSU	Mid stream urine
LFT	Liver function tests
Δ CA CX	Diagnosis: Cancer of cervix
For TAH & BSO	For total abdominal hysterectomy and bilateral salpingectomy (removal of uterus, tubes and ovaries)

Obstetrics

Obstetrics

Anatomy And Physiology

The mechanism by which fertilisation occurs is well understood. Once fertilised the egg (ovum) travels through the fallopian tube and reaches the uterus 3–4 days later. As it progresses through the tube it divides.

Terms relating to the cell/egg development:

- Morula – clump of cells
- Blastocle – appears few day later – next stage of development
- Trophoblast forms outside of blastocele – single layer of cells that develops into the placenta

Trophoblast

The inner cells of the blastocele develop into the foetus, amniotic fluid and umbilical cord. The inner cells separate into three layers, which in themselves form specific parts of the fetus.

These cells make the following:

a. Ectoderm (inner layer) forms the skin and neurological system
b. Mesoderm (middle section) forms the bones, muscles, heart and blood vessels
c. Endoderm (final layer) forms the mucus membranes and glands

In addition the amniotic cavity is formed which lies on the side of the ectoderm and fills with fluid.

A yolk sac forms at the side of the ectoderm to provide nourishment until trophoblast (placenta) can take over.

Placental function

a. Respiration – oxygen from maternal haemoglobin moves into fetal blood and removes CO_2
b. Nutrition – derived from the maternal diet

c. Excretion – mostly CO_2 and bilirubin
d. Protection
e. Endocrine – production of hormones, which assist with development.

Common hormones

- Human Chorionic Gonadatrophin
  HCG is produced in the chorionic villi and present in large quantities. Peak levels are apparent at 7–10 weeks. The production decreases as the pregnancy advances.
- Oestrogens
  Placenta takes over and large amount produced in pregnancy.
- Progesterone
  Large increase in quantities until immediately before labour when it reduces
  Measured in the urine in PREGNANEDIOL
- Human Placental Lactogen HPL.
  As HCG decreases so HPL increases

Other development issues

a. Amniotic fluid – this increases and allows for the growth and free movement of the fetus, protecting the fetus until the membranes are breached

b. Umbilical cord develops with three vessels from the placenta to the fetus. These are two arteries and one vein.

Growth and development of fetus

Weeks	Growth	Development
0–4	Rapid	Heart develops
4–8	Very Rapid	Heart and face, major organs Visible on ultra sound
8–12		Kidneys, sex apparent
12–16	Rapid skeletal growth	X-ray can see skeleton. Meconium apparent (waste product)
16–20		Fetal movement, finger nails
20–24		Organs capable of working, sleeping activity
24–28		Eyelids reopen respiratory movement
28–32		Fat and iron storage Testes are apparent
32–36		Increase in movement and nails
36–40		Contours reached and skull firm

Obstetric Records

1. Referral letter
2. Booking/clerking
3. Antenatal records
4. Labour Records
5. Puerperium records (Post natal)
6. Results and reports
7. CTG traces

The referral letter

Should indicate

- How many weeks pregnant (if possible)
- Estimated date of delivery
- Problems
- Whether first pregnancy
- Whether care is to be shared between GP and hospital.

Clerking

Details:

- Name
- Age
- Address
- Possible date of conception
- First pregnancy
- If not history of pregnancies (including unsuccessful or terminated pregnancies)
- Problems with any previous pregnancy
- Problems now (if any)
- Whether father around/ active in process
- General social history
- Any other medical condition – such as diabetes, cardiac problems

Obstetric History

How to read obstetric clerking records – common terms and expressions:

Gravida	G – Number of pregnancies
Para	P – Successful outcome (i.e. viable children/birth) e.g. G3P2 Three pregnancies but only two successful births e.g. G2P0 Two pregnancies but no successful births
Multigravida	Pregnant more than once
Multiparous	More than one child born
Nulliparous	No successful births
TOP	Termination of pregnancy
STOP	Spontaneous termination of pregnancy (miscarriage)
FTND	Full Term Normal Delivery
LSCS	Lower segment caesarean section (Can be elective or emergency)
A.P.H.	Antepartum haemorrhage (haemorrhage prior to delivery/during pregnancy)
P.P.H.	Post partum haemorrhage (haemorrhage after delivery of child/foetus)
EDC	Estimated date of confinement
EDD	Estimated date of delivery
Rh	Rhesus factor negative or positive factor which may affect future deliveries IF there is an incompatability between mother's factor and baby's. It is found in the blood. See antenatal tests.
VE	Vaginal examination
SROM	Spontaneous rupture of membrane
AROM	Artificial rupture of membranes

Timings

24/40	Pregnancy terminated/ended at 24 weeks or is currently 24 weeks pregnant
+2/40	Pregnancy continued two weeks late (i.e. 42 weeks)
–3/40	Premature birth – three weeks before estimated date of confinement
1st trimester	First 13 weeks of pregnancy
2nd trimester	Between 13 and 26 weeks of pregnancy
3rd/last trimester	27 to 39/40 weeks of pregnancy

Calculations

Usually 269 days from date of conception, this depends on the length of the usual cycle. A woman with a 28-day cycle will be within the region of 269 days. A women with a 35 day cycle will require an additional seven days to be added.

General terminology

Pica	Abnormal craving for foods
Cloasma	Darker pigmentation over forehead and cheeks (usually where dark complexion and exposure to sunlight)
Striae gravidarum	Stretch marks

Examination

A standard examination should include records of:

a. Height

b. Weight

c. Shoe Size – a size smaller than size 3 shoe may indicate possible problem with vaginal delivery (pelvis may be too small for this), though many obstetricians do not rely on this.

d. Blood pressure – to have baseline reading in case develops high blood pressure during pregnancy

e. Pulse

f. Urinalysis – Tests may be undertaken for:

  • Ketone – sign of increased work by mother
  • Protein – may be due to urinary tract infection
  • Glucose – check for the possible development of diabetes

g. Blood tests – Rh factor tests (see antenatal tests and investigations)

h. Blood test – haemoglobin – checking for anaemia – may require supplements. Repeated at a later stage in the pregnancy to check no anaemia before labour/delivery.

i. Other blood tests – VDRL (venereal disease research laboratory) tests for syphilis, HIV, Rubella (German measles) and alphafetoprotein tests (see antenatal tests and investigation)

j. Abdominal examination – aim is to check size of uterus, shape, ensure fetal movement, and estimate the period of gestation and to listen to fetal heart. Estimation of gestation – involves checking the height of the fetus/uterus. As the bulge of pregnancy appears nearer to the breasts so the gestational age can be estimated. In the last few weeks however the bulge appears to reduce as the fetus settles for the start of labour.

Antenatal records

On each visit the following should be checked:

a. Weight
b. Blood pressure
c. Urine
d. Lie (presentation) of fetus
e. Estimated gestation (age of fetus)
f. Whether any fetal movements have been felt or can be heard
g. Other notes – skin changes, problems with particular problems

Examination issues that may be recorded:

Presentation	Part of foetus which lies in the pelvic brim (down in the lower half of the abdomen). See below for presentation sections.
Denominator	The part of the body, which actually appears first • Vertex – Occiput (top of head) • Breech – Sacrum • Face – Mentum (see later)
Lie	Which way the fetus is lying in the uterus Determined by reviewing the long axis of the fetus (i.e. down the spine) and determining where it is in the uterus. Longitudinal lie – spine of fetus parallel to spine of mother. Can be: • Breech – where the head is at the top of the uterus • Vertex – where the head is at the bottom of the uterus Oblique lie – fetal spine is at angle of approximately 45 degrees Transverse lie – fetus at angle of approximately 90 degrees (i.e. lying sideways)
Fetal heart	CTG traces check for: • Baseline rate – whether it is satisfactory • Variability of rate • Response to contractions
Tests	Fetal Blood sampling: 1st stage labour – more than 7.25, action probably needed 2nd stage labour – more than 7.2 action needed

Ante partum tests and terminology

Rh – Rhesus factor

This is an antigen (substance capable of forming antibodies) which is present in blood. Most Caucasian people are rhesus positive because this is present. In some cases however the rhesus factor is not present and therefore the individual is considered rhesus negative.

Where here is an incompatibility between the maternal blood and the fetal blood there may be problems arising. The fetus may have the antigen because of the father but the mother may not. Where there is a leak of the fetal blood into the mother's blood stream her immune system will consider this foreign material and seek to destroy it. Put simply it does not recognise the antigen and considers it harmful.

The result is that in subsequent pregnancies the mother may form antibodies which if they cross over to the fetus can lead to haemolytic disease (conditions which can destroy red blood cells).

It is generally not a problem in a first pregnancy because it takes some time for recognition and development to occur. Subsequent pregnancies are a problem. In order to avoid the development of antibodies, rhesus negative mothers are screened at various times during pregnancy to check whether antibodies have developed. If levels appear significantly high, an amniocentesis may be considered and the fetus may need a transfusion while in the uterus. In some cases haemolytic disease in the fetus can be a serious situation and may require intensive care in the post natal period.

To avoid this situation arising, anti D immunoglobulin is given after delivery in rhesus negative women. This is an injected substance to prevent antibody formation.

GTT: Glucose tolerance test – (assist with diagnosis of possible diabetes). See, further, antenatal problems and conditions below.

AXR: Abdominal x-ray
On the whole x-rays are not used wherever pregnancy is confirmed or suspected unless absolutely necessary. It is sometimes necessary to undertake x-rays.

MSU: Mid stream urine – test for running urine for infection and glucose.

FBC: full blood count.

Alpha fetoprotein /MSAFP
Blood test on mother – usually between 16–18 weeks
Raised levels not always indicative of abnormalities
Low levels not always indicative of Downs

If raised level can do second test. If still raised then can:

Do ultrasound
Do amniocentesis

Amniocentesis
Removal of sample of amniotic fluid from around the placenta. Needle inserted through abdomen. Can ultrasound scan immediately.

Cardiotocograph (CTG trace)

Measures heart rate of fetus and contractions of labour.

Chorionic villus biopsy
Completed in first 13 weeks. Use of ultrasound to guide endoscope via vaginal or abdomen. Sample of chorionic villi taken which may indicate congenital abnormalities.

Cordocentesis
Sampling of fetal blood by inserting needle into cord.

Fetal Blood Sampling
Small sample of blood taken from scalp of fetus. Analysed immediately. Shows the pH of the blood and indicates whether there is a problem with the level of oxygen in the fetus.

Normal pH 7.35

< 7.25 may be problem depending on whether in labour and at what stage.

Fetoscopy

Endoscope inserted to check on visual appearance of fetus. Ultrasound scan can be immediately performed.

Can take blood samples to screen for various disorders

Ultrasound (USS)

High pitched sounds travel in straight line – sound wave passed through body and when it meets a structure – some of sound reflected back . Seen as a dot on screen – makes up an image.

Used for measurement of the fetus –

HC – head circumference
AC – abdominal circumference
CRL – crown rump length – from top to end of back
BPD – biparietal diameter – type of measurement of the skull.

Antenatal disorders and conditions

Threatened abortion

First sign of impending abortion. Marked by vaginal bleeding in early pregnancy.

Incomplete abortion

Where the fetus/part of fetus is expelled from the uterus, although some products of conception (fetus/placenta) remain.

Complete abortion

Where the entire fetus and placenta are expelled.

Missed abortion

Where the fetus dies in the uterus but is not expelled at that time. May be expelled later but often requires surgery to remove.

ERPC

Evacuation of the retained products of conception i.e. removal of the part/whole fetus and placenta which may not have been expelled during an incomplete or missed abortion.

Ectopic pregnancy

Pregnancy outside of the uterine cavity. May lead to:

- Salpingectomy – removal of fallopian tube
- Salpingotomy – making a hole in the tube to remove (in this case) the pregnancy with repair of the tube following this.

Hypertension

Increased blood pressure. Associated with:

- Pre eclampsia – a condition marked by hypertension, proteinuria (protein in the urine) and oedema (excessive fluid retention)
- Eclampsia – after 20 weeks of pregnancy with additional complication of fits.

Both conditions are potentially life threatening to mother and fetus/child.

Anaemia

Lower levels of iron in blood.

Diabetes

Four types found in pregnancy:

1. potential: No evidence found but either:

   i. family history
   ii. infant of large size
   iii. history of unexplained death from previous pregnancy

2. latent/gestational: developed during pregnancy
3. Chemical: abnormal glucose tolerance test result no symptoms
4. clinical diabetes insulin dependant diabetes mellitus (I D D M)

May result in:

- Hydramnios – excessive fluid surrounding the foetus in the uterus
- Pre eclampsia – as above
- Dystocia – fetus may be large resulting in an obstructed and difficult labour.
- Cephalo-pelvic disproportion – disproportion between the size of the head of the foetus and width of the pelvis – leading to possibly difficult birth.

Diabetes developed in pregnancy need not continue after pregnancy.

Ante partum haemorrhage (APH)

Bleeding from the genital tract between the 28th week of pregnancy and the onset of labour. Causes:

Placenta Praevia

Placenta planted in the lower segment of the uterus. Degrees of placenta praevia sometimes used

- Type 1: majority of placenta is attached to the upper segment of the uterus (i.e. where it should be). Some minor part of the segment is in the lower segment.

- Type 2: placenta is located both in upper and lower segment of the uterus. Part of placenta situated near the os. Vaginal delivery still possible.

- Type 3: placenta is located in the lower segment. Situated over the os but not central. Vaginal delivery not appropriate.

- Type 4: placenta located centrally over the os. Vaginal delivery not appropriate.

Abruptio Placenta

Haemorrhage resulting from premature separation of the placenta from the uterine wall. Haemorrhage can be either:

- Revealed   Haemorrhage apparent externally
- Concealed   Haemorrhage not apparent (usually because it occurs between the placenta and the uterine wall)

Degrees of Abruptio placenta:

- Mild – slight separation. Rest until 37 weeks if possible
- Moderate – up to 25% separation. Blood loss can be significant
- Severe – emergency situation requiring emergency caesarean section

Examination and History from patient:

- Abdominal examination – ? hard abdomen, soft, whether tender
- No vaginal or rectal examination
- No suppositories or enemas given
- Information required – amount of blood loss and when did it start? Degree of shock? Colour of blood? When pain started and whether continuous
- Check on fetus and heart beat

Wherever haemorrhage is a possibility the following tests and investigations should be looked for in the medical and nursing records:

1. Observations – pulse, blood pressure and temperature
2. A speculum examination may have taken place.
3. No vaginal or rectal examination
4. Bloods should be taken to check the haemoglobin level

Serious haemorrhage

1. Blood given and intravenous fluids provided
2. Insertion of central venous line
3. An accurate fluid balance chart measuring output and input
4. Clotting studies may be completed
5. Urinary catheter inserted

6. Ultrasound scan (possibility of concealed haemorrhage/placental location)
7. Careful monitoring of pulse and blood pressure.

Fetal tests:

1. CTG traces regular intervals
2. Preparation for caesarean section.

Labour Records

Stages of Labour

First: Onset to full dilatation of cervix
Second: Full dilatation through to expulsion
Third: Delivery of child to expulsion of placenta

Partogram
Single sheet which represents the progress of labour. Includes the fetal heart rate and dilatation of cervix.

Progress of labour measured by

- Dilatation of cervix
- Descent of fetus
- Effacement of cervix
- Fetal heart
- Checking of position and which part presents – i.e. review of position, presentation and denominator
- Frequency of contractions
- Normal observations – pulse, blood pressure etc

Dilatation of cervix

Expressed as Cx 0–10 cm scale. Usually made in two stages:

- Latent 0–3 cm generally. Takes 2/3 time of the actual labour
- Active 3–10 cm Takes 1/3 time of the labour (approximately)

It is actually the external os (the lower part of the cervix) which is measured.

10 cm is the maximum.

Descent of part

Movement of the fetus downwards during labour.

Measured along scale in two stages.

- The first from the pelvic brim to the ischial spine . This is defined as starting at −5 cm and progressing downwards to 0 which is equal to the ischial spine.
- The second stage is from the ischial spine through to the final appearance. This is defined as starting at 0 and progressing towards +5 cm.

The ischial spine is a part of the pelvis, which is used to determine the progress of labour. It is the placed just behind the thickest part of the pelvis.

Effacement – process by which the cervix gets takes up and dilates during labour to allow for the passage of the fetus. It thins and moves up the sides. Occurs at the same time as dilatation.

The fetal heart rate

FHH: fetal heart heard
FHHR   fetal heart heard and reactive

Usually 110–160 beats per minute (b.p.m.)

- Decelerations: **TYPE I/early**
  Deceleration in heart rate commences with the onset of contraction and is normal with completion of contraction. Usually associated with head or cord compression.

- Decelerations: **TYPE II/late**
  After contraction occurs. Not normal level until 20 seconds or so after completion.

Presentation

This is the area of the body which comes through the vaginal canal
first.

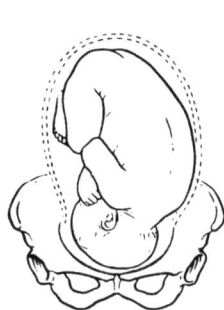

Vertex Head first	Brow Top of brow	Face Head first – neck bent down

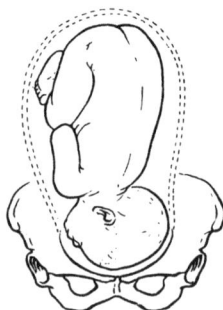

Breech Buttocks first	Shoulder, Shoulder first	Shoulder, Shoulder first

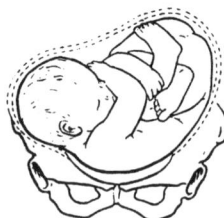

Varieties of cephalic or head presentation

Position and denominator

The denominator is a reference point to establish the position of the fetus. each type of presentation has a different denominator: for example

- Vertex – head first delivery – back of the head is the denominator (Occiput)
- Breech buttocks first – the sacrum is the denominator

By using the denominator the position of the fetus can be stablished. The position is simply where the denominator is in relation to the pelvic brim.

1. The position will be   either left or right   L or R

2. The position will be

vertex –	occiput	O
breech –	sacrum	S
face	mentum	M

3. The position will be

posterior	at the back	P
lateral	side of the brim	L
anterior	at the front	A

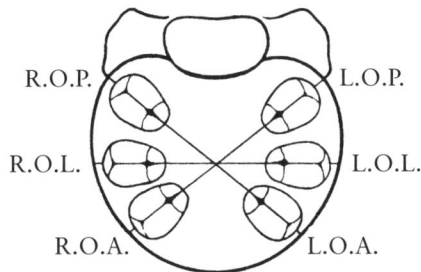

Diagrammatic representation of the six vertex
positions and their relative frequency

Vertex: top of head is part noted first through cervix	
Left occipito-anterior (LOA)	Right occipito-anterior (ROA)
Left occipito-transverse (LOT) -lateral (LOL)	Right occipito-transverse (ROT) -lateral (ROL)
Left occipito-posterior (LOP)	Right occipito-posterior (ROP)
Face: face shows first through the cervix	
Left mento-anterior (LMA)	Right mento-anterior (RMA)
Left mento-transverse (LMT) -lateral (LML)	Right mento-transverse (RMT) -lateral (RML)
Left mento-posterior (LMP)	Right mento-posterior (RMP)
Breech: part which shows through the cervix is foot or buttocks	
Frank	Flexed
Footling	Breech deliveries are usually described as: • Left sacrum – anterior • Left sacrum – transverse/lateral • Left sacrum-posterior • Right sacral-anterior • Right sacral transverse/lateral • Right sacral posterior
Shoulder deliveries: types are	
Dorsum	Acromium process

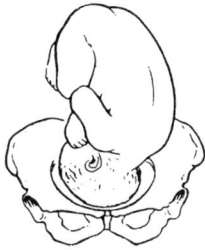

Left
occipito-anterior

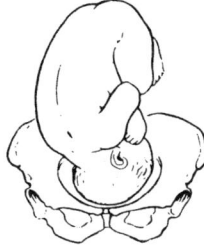

Right
occipito-anterior

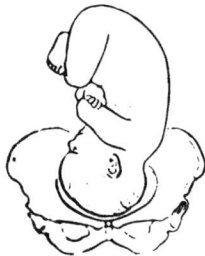

Left
occipitolateral

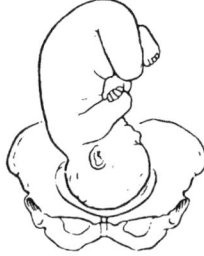

Right
occipitolateral

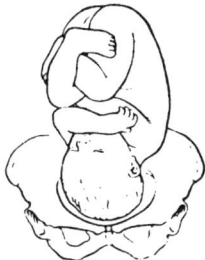

Left
occipitoposterior

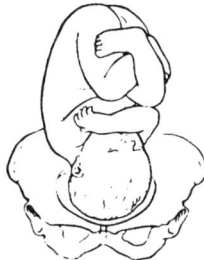

Right
occipitoposterior

Six positions in vertex presentation

Contractions

Measured by minutes

- 1 in every 15 minutes – 1 in 15
- 1 in every three minutes 1 in 3
- More frequent – more likely delivery approaching

Maternal checks

Check for blood pressure and pulse, temperature and urine tests as necessary.

Blood pressure should be undertaken frequently to check for possible signs of eclampsia.

Types of delivery

Vaginal delivery

Can be normal i.e.: without assistance of any equipment.
Can be assisted using:

- Ventouse – type of cap, which inserts onto the head of the fetus and allows (through the use of suction) the application of more force to pull the fetus out of the vagina.
- Forceps – different types but essentially they fit round the two sides of the fetal head and allow for the head to be brought out.

If vaginal delivery is not possible then surgery is required.

Lower segment caesarean section (L S C S)

Can be elective (booked) or emergency
Surgical intervention to open the uterus and remove infant and placenta.

Post natal problems: problems in the puerperium

Problem	Signs	Treatment and issues
Post partum haemorrhage (Mother has a haemorrhage after the delivery) – can be defined as primary (immediately after) or secondary (24 hours or more later)	May be visible bleeding. Deterioration in mother's condition, increasing thready pulse, decreasing blood pressure, sweatiness, anxiety and cyanosis (blue colour) or pallor (pale appearance) cool. Can also detect where large uterus filled with blood	Depends on cause but the following are usually completed: • Medications to ensure uterus is contracted. • Delivery of the placenta and clots • Intravenous fluids and blood products • Full blood count • Surgical repair if necessary • Hysterectomy if the uterus has ruptured.
Shock – mother's circulatory system cannot meet the demands for oxygen, removal or waste products and nutrition	Increasing thready pulse. Decreasing blood pressure at later stages. Rapid respirations but shallow in nature. Reduction in the production of urine	Treat cause (can be haemorrhage or allergic reaction for example). Ensure breathing and give oxygen. Check for signs of haemorrhage. Intravenous fluids. Insert CVP line (central venous pressure) – needle into the central veins to detect the pressure in the blood system)
Inversion: uterus turns inside out	Signs of shock above	Placenta should not be removed until uterus back in position. Gentle positioning back manually if possible. Surgery if required. All preparations for surgery

Problem	Signs	Treatment and issues
Tears are defined as: • 1st degree (vaginal skin and the top layer of the perineum) • 2nd degree – deeper tissue layers involved • 3rd degree – edges of the anus have become involved • 4th degree – anal sphincter (muscle) has become involved	Usually evident from appearance	Third and fourth degree usually require surgery and skilled care to suture wounds. Can develop clots and infection – careful checking and cleaning to maintain wound repair
Pyrexia (increased temperature)	Due to infection often. Increasing temperature levels	Full examination. Swabs from all relevant areas for culture and sensitivity. Urine tests for same. Full blood count. Once organism identified – antibiotics and anti pyrexials (to reduce temperature)
Psychiatric conditions: • Depression • Psychosis	• Depression – feel fine in morning but deteriorate through day. Problems coping with baby • Psychosis – mania or hallucinations, strange behaviour	Reduce stress, support mother and medications. If early detection – care at home. If prolonged problem or serious in nature may require admission. Psychosis: Admit to psychiatric unit. Medications (depending on nature of psychosis) and full psychiatric care.

Apgar scores

Means by which the condition of a child at birth is recorded. Five areas are reviewed and scored accordingly. Usually taken as a number from 0–10 depending on the condition.

	0	1	2
Colour	White	Blue	Pink
Tone	Flaccid	Rigid	Normal
Pulse	Impalpable	<100 b.p.m	>100 b.p.m
Respiration	Absent	Irregular	Regular
Response	Absent	Poor	Normal

Usually taken a one minute and five minutes. Where problems are apparent (i.e. low reading) will also be noted at ten minutes.

Clinical records – clerking

Notes	Meaning
35 yrs, multigravida	35 years of age, previous pregnancies
P3 G2 TOP 1983	Three pregnancies, 2 successful, one termination of pregnancy in 1983
FTND Male 8	Full term normal delivery boy aged 8
FTND female 5	Full term normal delivery girl aged 5
LMP: 4/9/99	Last menstrual period September
Usually 4-5/7 reg	Usually regular 4–5 days
?8/40	Now 8 weeks into pregnancy (estimation)
EDD 7/6/2000	Estimated date of delivery – 7th June
PMx – FTND 91 – PPH	Past medial history – delivery in 91 – post partum haemorrhage
FTND 94 – PPH	Delivery in 94 same problem
IDDM –	Is an insulin dependant diabetic
Married. Father in attendance	As indicated
O/E obese, shoe size 3	On examination is obese with small shoe size
BP 120/75 Pulse 85	Blood pressure and pulse readings
VE NAD	Vaginal examination – nothing abnormal detected

Notes	Meaning
Uterus - 8/40	Uterus on examination consistent with 8 weeks pregnancy
For shared care	For shared care between hospital and GP
MSU	For mid stream urine test
FBC/VDRL/HIV/Rh	For blood tests – full blood count, screening for syphilis and HIV, check on rhesus factor
ANC 4/52	Next appointment @ ante natal clinic – 4 weeks time

Labour Records

12:00	Multigravida. Admitted for ARM & induction. 2+ contractions 1 in 15	Previous pregnancies. Admitted for artificial rupture of membranes and induction of labour. Forty two weeks pregnancy – two weeks over due. Contractions one in every 15 minutes.
12:20	ARM FHHR CTG commenced	Artificial rupture of membranes. Fetal heart heard and reactive. Cardiotacograph commenced.
12:30	Type I dec - S/B Dr Obst	Type I decelerations noted. Seen by Dr Obstetrics.
12:45	VE - Cx 5 cms -1 1 in 3 Contractions	Vaginal examination undertaken. Traveling through at level where head 1 cm above the ischial spine. Contractions one in every three minutes. Cervix 5 cm dilated
13:00	Type II dec. S/B DR Obs (reg) FBS - 7.15 D/w Ms Obs (SR) - for LSCS emergency. Anaesthetist fast bleep	Type II decelerations noted. Seen by Dr Registrar Obstetrics. Fetal Blood sample – notes acidosis (pH 7.15). Discussed with Ms Senior Registrar Obstetrics. For emergency caesarean section. Anaesthetist called.

13:30	Emergency LSCS. Pfanesteil. Male 2 @ 1 minute, 6 @ 5 minutes. Paed present.	Emergency lower segment caesarean section. Pfannesteil incision (along the line of the pubic bone). Delivery of male infant. Apgar scores 2 at one minute, 6 at five minutes. Paediatrician in attendance
14:15	Transfer PNW IV Syntocinon - Baby - SCBU	Transferred to postnatal ward. Intravenous infusion commenced. Syntocinon given. Infant to special care baby unit

How to Obtain Medical Records

How to Obtain Medical Records

Who owns the records?

The common belief is that the patient owns the records*. This is not the case. Ownership is usually as follows:

a. NHS Hospital

NHS Trust

b. GP (NHS)

Local FHSA (Family Services Health Authority) – usually part of Primary Care Trust

c. Private Hospital

Consultant in charge of care

d. Scans (private)

Client/Patient

e. Dental (NHS)

Local Family Dental Services Authority (usually same as GP) – usually Trust

f. Dental private

Dentist

g. Optician

Optician

h. Physiotherapy (NHS)

NHS Trust

i. Physiotherapy (private)

Physiotherapist

J   Counsellor(NHS)

Either FHSA (if attached to NHS GP) or NHS Trust

k. Counsellor (private)

Counsellor
Most are private even if attached to GP Practice

---

* For a more general discussion of the issue see *Patient Confidentiality*, EMIS Professional Publishing, 2002.

The Access to Health Records Act 1990

This act allows for patients to have access to their records after November 1, 1991. The patient does not have to give reasons for the request and can authorise any other individual to apply for access on his or her behalf including a solicitor. No differential charging rates can be applied.

Fees and charges

The Access to Health Records Act 1990 stipulates a maximum fee of £10. Additional charges which can be levied are for photocopying and postage. Any charges for copying should include cost of staff time. The BMA usually have a recommended rate for photocopying (currently 33p per sheet).

Medical records departments and GP practices are still charging a standard administration fee for records. This is no longer appropriate.

The NHS executive guidance provided by the Department of Health confirms that the request for records to for the purposes of potential or actual litigation whether against the trust or a third party is perfectly acceptable.

Fewer medical practices are willing to forward the original records due to the number of records which have in the past become lost as a result. GP practices in particular however are notorious for failing to comply with requests for the records to be copied onto single sided A4 paper.

Applied to records after November 1991. Records prior to that time are subject to the usual whims and arrangements of the hospitals and GPs.

The Data Protection Act 1998

This Act came into force on March 1, 2000. It applies to all records regardless of date.

The Act applies to all structured records about persons still living. The records can be manual and computerised.

The Act gives rights to individuals in respect of personal data held about them by others. These rights include:

1. Right of access

2. Right to prevent processing likely to cause damage or distress

3. Right to take action for compensation if the individual suffers damage by any contravention of the Act by the data controller

4. Right to take action to rectify, block, erase or destroy inaccurate data

5. Can request Commissioner assesses whether the Act has been contravened.

The *Data Controller* is the person who decides how and why collation of data is completed and the person who carries out the procedure.
  Under schedule 1:

1. all data must be processed for lawful purposes
2. all data must be accurate
3. all data must be up to date

Schedule 2 sets out preconditions including the consent of the individual concerned.
  Schedule 3 states that sensitive material has additional requirements as follows:

1. express consent of individual concerned
2. legal requirement for employment purposes
3. protection of interests of third party
4. protection of interests of person concerned
5. administration of justice
6. conduct of proceedings.

Right of Access

The individual is entitled upon payment of a fee and by written request under section 7.

(a) to be informed by the data controller whether they or someone else is processing personal data concerning the individual.

(b) To be provided with a description of

1. data held
2. purposes it is being processed
3. those to whom it has been disclosed
4. Those to whom it may be disclosed

(c) To be provided in an intelligible form

1. All information processed
2. Information as to source of data (subject to certain restrictions)
3. Where a decision is taken on that data which may affect work, credit, concerns their reliability or conduct additional information on the thought process should be included.

Fees

The data controller can charge a fee, which is currently defined as £50 maximum. It was anticipated that this would change but this fee has been retained for the moment.

Must supply within 40 days of request.

If the data controller does not supply within 40 days the fee is refundable.

The Data Protection (Subject Access Modification) (Health) Order 1999

This order modifies the Data Protection Act 1998

Terms

Under the Order a health professional is:–

- the one most recently responsible for clinical care to which request relates OR
- Where more than one – the one most suitable to advise on matters to which information which is the subject of the request relates OR

- A health professional with the necessary experience and qualifications

The information covered by the order relates to any personal data. This includes information as to the physical or mental health of the individual concerned.

Exemptions from section 7 (access)

The Data Protection (Subject Access Modification)(Health) Order 1999 provides exemptions from access under section 7 of the Data Protection Act 1998 where access would be likely to causes serious harm to the mental health or condition of the individual concerned or any other person. Prior to any decision being taken however any data controller who is not a health professional must seek the opinion of the appropriate health professional or if there are none available then a suitably qualified and experienced health professional.

The obligation to consult does not apply where the individual had already seen the information or is aware of it. It also does not apply where an opinion was sought prior to the request being made by the individual concerned.

Care should be taken when applying for records for children or those whose affairs are managed by an individual appointed by the court because of incapability (with the exception of Scotland where differing rules apply). A person with parental responsibility, or appointed by the court to manage the affairs of a person who is incapable, can prevent disclosure if they believe the data was collated in the expectation of, or, at the express request of the individual concerned, that it would not be disclosed. Likewise in a person without disability disclosure can be prevented if the data were collected in the expectation of or at the express request that it would not be disclosed.

An exemption from section 7 is restricted where a third party identity would be disclosed in health records and the third party is a health professional who has either compiled the record or been involved in the care of the individual as a health professional unless there is a risk of serious physical or mental harm to the health professional concerned.

Disclosure under the Civil Procedure Rules

The familiar pre-action discovery rules of section 33 (2) of the Supreme Court Act 1981 or section 52 (2) of the County Courts Act 1984 have been altered by the Civil Procedure Rules.

Rule 25(1)(1) of the Civil Procedure Rules allows the court to grant a number of interim remedies including:

(i) an order under section 33 S.C.A. 1981 or section 52 C.C.A. 1984 (order for disclosure of documents or inspection of property before a claim is made);

(j) an order under section 34 S.C.A. 1981 or section 53 C.C.A. 1984 (order in certain proceedings for disclosure of documents or inspection of property against a non party.

The power to make both orders is found within C.P.R. 31.16 and 31.17 respectively.

CPR 31.16

CPR **31.16** allows for the following:

The court can make an order for disclosure before proceedings start where:

- Both the respondent and applicant are likely to be party to subsequent proceedings (s.(3)(*a*) or (*b*))

  and

  If proceedings had started the respondent would have a duty under standard disclosure to disclosure the documents concerned (s.(3)(*c*))

  and

- disclosure before proceedings have started are desirable because they may:

  * dispose fairly of the anticipated proceedings (s.(3)(*d*)(i))
  * assist resolution of the dispute without proceedings (s.(3)(*d*)(ii))
  * or save costs (s.(3)(*d*)(iii))

The order must:

- specify the documents or classes of documents which must be disclosed (s.(4)(*a*))

If the respondent no longer has in his control certain documents or claims a right or duty to withhold inspection these must be specified.

- The order may require the respondent to indicate which documents are no longer in the respondent's control (s.(4)(*b*)(i)) or

- documents which he claims he has a right or duty to withhold (s.(4)(*b*)(ii))

Further the order may:

- require the respondent to indicate what has happened to the documents no longer in his control (s.(5)(*a*))

    and

- detail the time and place for disclosure and inspection s.(5)(*b*)

CPR 31.17

Orders for disclosure against a non party

OPR 31.17 allows for the following:

The court can only make the order where:

- the documents concerned are likely to support he case of the applicant or adversely affect he case of another party. (s.(3)(*a*))

- Disclosure is necessary to dispose of the claim fairly or to save costs (s.(3)(*b*))

An order must:

- specify the documents or class of documents to be disclosed (s.(4)(*a*))

- require the respondent to specify any documents

- which are no longer in his control (s.(4)(*b*)(i))

- where he claims a duty or right to withhold inspection (s.(4)(*b*)(ii))

The order may require:

- The respondent to indicate what has happened to any documents which are no longer in his control (s.(5)(*a*))

- specify the time and place for disclosure (s.(5)(*b*))

The normal order will provide for standard disclosure. It is still possible to apply for specific disclosure using Rule 31.12.

The Protocols

Both personal injury and clinical negligence actions now have protocols which should be completed. It is anticipated that this will spread to other areas of practice in due course.

The protocols are aimed at providing as much information as possible to both sides prior to commencement of proceedings. The earlier the information is available the more likely it is for matters to settle.

Aside from the usual requirements of the protocols there is an obligation to provide copy medical records as soon as possible to allow for the investigation of the matter. It is suggested that the sorted records may be provided (using a duplicate bundle) with the letter of claim detailing the appropriate references.

The Protocols have also developed forms for application on behalf of a patient for hospital records for use when court proceedings are contemplated. There are also forms in response. The use of the forms is voluntary at present. Specimens can be found in the Protocol sections of the C.P.R and should reduce the need for covering detailed letters.

Requests for records should take no more than 40 days. Records should be provided by health care providers in the following form:

- All documents should be legible and complete
- copying should be at least 100% size
- documents larger than A4 (e g ITU charts) should be copied onto A3 if possible or reduced only if they remain readable.
- Documents should only be copied on one side of paper unless the original is two sided.
- The papers should not be unnecessarily shuffled or bound.
- Holes should not be made in copied papers.

Appendices

Appendix 1

Abbreviations

Please note that some abbreviations are used for more than one purpose depending on the context.

Aa	OF EACH
A	ATTENDANCE
AAW	ALIVE AND WELL
ABx	ANTIBIOTICS
Ac	BEFORE FOOD
AC	ABDOMINAL CIRCUMFERENCE
Add	ADDUCTION
A & E	ACCDIENT & EMERGENCY
AE	AIR ENTRY
AF	ATRIAL FIBRILLIATION
AFB	ALFA FETO PROTEIN
AFB	ACID FAST BACILLI
AFB	ALFA FETA PROTEIN
AID	ARTIFICIAL INSEMINATION DONOR
AIDS	ACQUIRED IMMUNO DEFICIENCY SYNDROME
Aj	ANKLE JERK
ALT DIE	ALTERNATIVE DAYS
ALT NOCTE	ALTERNATIVE NIGHTS
AN	ANTENATAL
ANS	AUTONOMIC NERVOUS SYSTEM
AP	ANTERIO-POSTERIOR, ARTIFICIAL PNEUMOTHORAX
APH	ANTE PARTUM HAEMORRHAGE
App	APPLICATIONS
AQ	WATER
ARDS	ADULT RESPIRATORY DISTRESS SYNDROME
ARM	ARTIFICAL RUPTURE OF MEMBRANES
AS	ANKYLOSING SPONDYLOSIS
ASD	ATRIAL SEPTAL DEFECT
A/v	ANTEVERTED
AVS	AORTIC VALVE STENOSIS
A&W	ALIVE AND WELL
AXR	ABDOMINAL X-RAY
Ba	BARIUM
BaE	BARIUM ENEMA

BaM	BARIUM MEAL
BBB	BUNDLE BRANCH BLOCK
BD	TWICE A DAY
BID	BROUGHT IN DEAD
BP	BLOOD PRESSURE
BMR	BASAL METABOLIC RATE
BO	BOWELS OPEN
BPD	BIPARIETAL DIAMETER
BS	BOWEL SOUNDS, BREATH SOUNDS, BLOOD SUGAR
BSO	BILATERAL SALPING-OOPHRECTOMY (GYNAE)
c	CUM – WITH
$C_2 H_2OH$	ALCOHOL
Ca	CANCER OR CALCIUM
CABG	CORONERY ARTERY BY PASS GRAFT
CCU	CORONARY CARE UNIT
CDH	CONGENITAL DISLOCATION OF THE HIP
CIN	MEASUREMENT OF CERVICAL CANCER
CITU	CORONARY INTENSIVE CARE UNIT
CMV	CYTOMEGALOVIRUS
CNS	CENTRAL NERVOUS SYSTEM
CO	CARBON MONOXIDE/COMPLAINING OF
CO_2	CARBON DIOXIDE
COAD	CHRONIC OBSTRUCTIVE AIRWAYS DISEASE
CPD	CEPHALO PARIETAL DISPROPORTION
CPR	CARDIOPULMONARY RESUSCITATION
C & S	CULTURE AND SENSITIVITY
CRC	CROWN RUMP CIRCUMFERENCE
CSF	CEREBRO SPINAL FLUID
CT/CAT	COMPUTED AXIAL TOMOGRAPH (CAT SCAN)
CTG	CARDIOTOCOGRAPH
CVA	CEREBRAL VASCULAR DISEASE (STROKE)
CVP	CENTRAL VENOUS PRESSURE
CVS	CARDIO VASCULAR SYSTEM, CHORIONIC VILLUS SAMPLING
Cx	CERVIX
CXR	CHEST X-RAY
D & C	DILATATION AND CURETTAGE
DIC	DISSEMINATED INTRAVESCULAR COAGULATION
DNA	DID NOT ATTEND
DOA	DEAD ON ARRIVAL
DOB	DATE OF BIRTH
D & V	DIARRHOEA AND VOMITING
DT	DELIRIUM TREMENS
DU	DUODENAL ULCER
DVT	DEEP VEIN THROMBOSIS
DW	DISCUSSED WITH

Dx	DIAGNOSIS
EC	ENTERIC COATED
ECG	ELECTROCARDIOGRAM
EDC	ESTIMATED DATE OF CONFINEMENT
EDD	ESTIMATED DATE OF DELIVERY
E E G	ELECTRO ENCEPHAOLOGRAM/GRAPH
EMG	ELECTROMYOGRAPH
EMU	EARLY MORNING URINE
ENT	EAR NOSE AND THROAT
ERCP	ENDOSCOPIC RETROGRADE CHOLANGI PANCREATOGRAPHY
ERPC	EVACUATION OF RETAINED PRODUCTS OF CONCEPTION
ESR	ERYTHROCYTE SEDIMENTATION RATE
EUA	EXAMINATION UNDER ANAESTHETIC
FB	FOREIGN BODY
FBC	FULL BLOOD COUNT
FBS	FETAL BLOOD SAPMLE
FH/FHx	FAMILY HISTORY
FHH	FETAL HEART HEARD
FHR	FETAL HEART RATE
FHHR	FETAL HEART HEARD AND REACTIVE
FMF	FETAL MOVEMENTS FELT
FRC	FUNCTIONAL RESIDUAL CAPACITY
FSE	FETAL SCALP ELECTRODE
FSH	FOLLICLE STIMULATING HORMONE
FTND	FULL TERM NORMAL DELIVERY
FTT	FAILURE TO THRIVE
GA	GENERAL ANAESTHETIC
GI	GASTRO INTESTINAL
GOK	GOD ONLY KNOWS
GTT	GLUCOSE TOLERANCE TEST
GU	GENITO URINARY, GASTRIC ULCER
GUT	GENITO URINARY TRACT
HB	HAEMOGLOBIN
HC	HEAD CIRCUMFERENCE
HCG	HUMAN CHORIONIC GONADATROPHIN HORMONE
HCO_3	BICARBONATE
HDU	HIGH DEPENDENCY UNIT
HNPU	HAS NOT PASSED URINE
HPC	HISTORY OF PRESENT COMPLAINT
HRT	HORMONE REPLACEMENT THERAPY
HS	HEART SOUNDS
HSG	HYSTEROSALPINGOGRAM

HVS	HIGH VAGINAL SWAB
Hx	HISTORY
IDDM	INSULIN DEPENDENT DIABETES MELLITUS
IHD	ISCHAEMIC HEART DISEASE
IM	INTRAMUSCULAR
ISQ	IN STATUS QUO
IT	INTRA THECAL
IUCD	INTRA UTERINE CONTRACEPTIVE DEVICE
IV	INTRAVENOUS
IVF	IN-VITRO FERTILISATION
IVI	INTRA VENOUS INFUSION
IVP	INTRAVENOUS PYELOGRAM
IVU	INTRAVENOUS UROGRAM
K	POTASSIUM
KJ	KNEE JERK
KO	KNOCKED OUT
L	LITRE
LA	LOCAL ANAESTHETIC
LFT	LIVER FUNCTION TESTS
LIF	LEFT ILIAC FOSSA
LMP	LAST MENSTRUAL PERIOD
LN	LYMPH NODE
LOA	LEFT OCCIPUT ANTERIOR
LOC	LOSS OF CONSCIOUSNESS
LOL	LEFT OCCIPUT LATERAL
LOP	LEFT OCCIPUT POSTERIOR
LP	LUMBAR PUNCTURE
LRTI	LOWER RESPIRATORY TRACT INFECTION
LSCS	LOWER SEGMENT CAESAREAN SECTION
LSK	LIVER SPLEEN AND KIDNEYS
LVF	LEFT VENTRICULAR FAILURE
MANE	MORNING
MCH	MEAN CELL HAEMOGLOBIN
MCHC	MEAN CELL HAEMOGLOBIN CONCENTRATION
MCL	MID CLAVICULAR LINE
M C & S	MICROSCOPY CULTURE AND SENSITIVITY
Mg	MILLIGRAM
MI	MYOCARDIAL INFRACTION
ML	MILILITRE
MRI	MAGNETIC RESONANCE IMAGING
MRSA	MULTI RESISTANT STAPHYLOCCUS AUREUS OR MENTHIRILLIN RESISTANT
MSU	MID STREAM URINE
MUA	MANIPULATION UNDER ANAESTHETIC
MVS	MITRAL VALVE STENOSIS

NAD	NOTHING ABNORMAL DETECTED
NAI	NON ACCIDENTAL INJURY
NBI	NO BONY INJURY
NBM	NIL BY MOUTH
NIDDM	NON INSULIN DEPENDANT DIABETIES (MELLITUS)
NOAD	NO OTHER ABNORMALITY DETECTED
NOCTE	NIGHT
NOF	NECK OF FEMUR
NSAID	NON STEROIDAL ANTI INFLAMMATORIES
O_2	OXYGEN
OA	OSTEOARTHRITIS
OD	ONCE A DAY
OE	ON EXAMINATION
oe	EVERY EVENING
OGD	OESOPHAGEAL GASTRO DUODENOSCOPY
om	EVERY MORNING
OP	OCCIPUT POSTERIOR
OPA	OUT PATIENT APPOINTMENT
OPD	OUT PATIENT DEPARTMENT
P	PULSE
PA	PROTRUSIO ACETABULI/PULMONARY ARTERY
pc	AFTER EATING
PCO	PATIENT COMPLAINING OF
PCV	PACKED CELLS VOLUME
PDA	PATENT DUCTUS ARTERIOSUS
PERLA	PUPILS EQUAL AND REACTING TO LIGHT AND ACCOMODATION
PE	PULMONARY EMBOLISM
PH/PHx	PAST HISTORY
PID	PELVIC INFLAMMATORY DISEASE
PMH/PMHX	PAST MEDICAL HISTORY
PN	POST NATAL
PND	POST NASAL DRIP/POST NATAL DEPRESSION
PNS	PERIPHERAL NERVOUS SYSTEM
PO	TAKEN ORALLY
POP	PLASTER OF PARIS
PPH	POST PARTUM HAEMORRHAGE
PR	BY RECTUM
PRN	AS NEEDED
PTT/PT	PROTHROMBIN TIME
PU	PASSED URINE
PUO	PYREXIA OF UNKNOWN ORIGIN
PV	BY VAGINA
PXR	PELVIC X-RAY
QDS	FOUR TIMES A DAY

RA	RHEUMATOID ARTHRITIS
RBC	RED BLOOD CELL COUNT
RDS	RESPIRATORY DISTRESS SYNDROME
REM	RAPID EYE MOVEMENTS
Rh	RHESUS
RHF	RIGHT HEART FAILURE
RIH	RIGHT INGUINAL HERNIA
ROA	RIGHT OCCIPUT ANTERIOR
ROL	RIGHT OCCIPUT LATERAL
ROM	RANGE OF MOVEMENT
ROP	RIGHT OCCIPUT POSTERIOR
RS	RESPIRATORY SYSTEM
RTA	ROAD TRAFFIC ACCIDENT
RTI	RESPIRATORY TRACT INFECTION
RV	RIGHT VENTRICLE, RESIDUAL VOLUME
S_{1-4}	HEART SOUNDS
SAH	SUB ARACHNOID HAEMORRHAGE
SB	SINUS BRADYCARDIA, SEEN BY, STILL BIRTH
SCAN	SUSPECTED STILL BIRTH OR NEGLECT
SIDS	SUDDEN INFANT DEATH SYNDROME
SH/SHx	SOCIAL HISTORY
SOB	SHORTNESS OF BREATH
SOBOE	SHORTNESS OF BREATH ON EXERTION
SOL	SPACE OCCUPYING LESION
SR	SINUS RHYTHM
SROM	SPONTANEOUS RUPTURE OF MEMBRANES
ST	SINUS TACHYCARDIA
STOP	SPONTANEOUS TERMINATION OF PREGNANCY
SVC	SUPERIOR VENA CAVA
SVD	SPONTANEOUS VAGINAL DELIVERY
SVT	SUPRA VENTRICULAR TACHYCARDIA
T & A	TONSILLECTOMY AND ADENOIDECTOMY
TATT	TIRED ALL THE TIME
TAH	TOTAL ABDOMINAL HYSTERECTMY
TCA	TO COME AGAIN
TCI	TO COME IN
TDS	THREE TIMES A DAY
THR	TOTAL HIP REPLACEMENT
TIA	TRANSIENT ISCHAEMIC ATTACK
TID	THREE TIMES A DAY
TJ	TRICEPS JERK
TKR	TOTAL KNEE REPLACEMENT
TLC	TENDER LOVING CARE, TOTAL LUNG CAPACITY
TLE	TEMPORAL LOBE EPILEPSY
TOP	TERMINATION OF PREGNANCY
TPR	TEMPERATURE PULSE AND RESPIRATIONS

TSH	THYROID STIMULATING HORMONE
TTA	TO TAKE AWAY
TTO	TO TAKE OUT
TV	TIDAL VOLUME
U & E	UREA AND ELECTROLYTES
UG	URINOGENITAL
URTI	UPPER RESPITAORY TRACT INFECTION
USS	ULTRA SOUND SCAN
VC	VITAL CAPACITY
VD	VAGINAL DELIVERY
VE	VAGINAL EXAMINATION
VF	VENTRICULAR FIBRILLIATION
VSD	VENTRICULAR SEPTAL DEFECT
VT	VENTRICULAR TACHYCARDIA
V/V	VAGINA AND VULVA
Vx	VERTEX
WBC	WHITE BLOOD COUNT
WR	WARD ROUND
XRY	X RAY EXAMINATION

Appendix 2

Common hieroglyphics

Many	+ + +
Diagnosis	Δ
Differential diagnosis	ΔΔ
Increase	↑
Decrease	↓
Treatment	℞
Psychiatric	ψ
No	°
Constant	→
Less than	<
More than	>
Query	?
One month	1/12
Two weeks	2/52
Three days	3/7
Woman	♀
Man	♂
Fracture	#

Appendix 3

Medical Terminology

A(N)	ABSENCE OF
ACOU/ACU	HEAR
ADEN/ADENO	GLAND
AEMIA	BLOOD
AER/AERO	AIR
ALG	PAIN
ANDR/ANDRO	MAN
ANGIO	VESSEL
ANKLY/O	CROOKED OR CURVED
ANTE	BEFORE
ANTER/ANTERIOR	IN FRONT
ANTI	AGAINST
APGAR	MEANS OF SCORING CONDITION OF NEW BORN INFANT
ARTERIO	ARTERY/ARTERIAL
ARTHRO	JOINT
AUDI/AUDIO	HEARING
AUR/AURI	EAR
BI	TWO/TWICE
BRADY	SLOW
CARCIN/CARCINO	CANCER
CARDI/CARDIO	HEART
CEPHAL	HEAD
CEREBRO/AL	BRAIN
CHOL/CHOLE	BILE OR GALL BLADDER
CHONDRO	CARTILAGE
CONTRA	AGAINST/COUNTER TO
COSTO/COSTAL	RIB
CYANO	BLUE
DERMATO	SKIN
DIPLO	DOUBLE
DYS	FAULTY
ECTOMY	EXCISION
EFFUSION	REMOVAL OF FLUID IN A JOINT
END/ENDO	INSIDE
ENTERO	INTESTINE

ESR	ERYTHROCYTE SEDIMENTATION RATE ESR
EXTENSION	MOVING A JOINT IN A STRAIGHT LINE
EXTERNAL	OUTER SIDE
FEMUR	THIGH BONE
FLACCID	LIMPNESS NORMALLY ASSOCIATED WITH MUSCLES
FOSSA	DEPRESSION OR FURROW
FRACTURE	BROKEN BONE
FRONTAL	AT THE FRONT OF THE HEAD
GASTRO	STOMACH
GLASGOW COMA SCALE	MEANS TO TEST CONSCIOUSNESS LEVELS
GYN	FEMALE
HAEM	BLOOD
HEMI	HALF
HEPATO	LIVER
HISTO	TISSUE
HYDRO	WATER
HYPER	EXCESSIVE OR HIGH
HYPO	DEFICIENT OR LOW
HYSTER/O	UTERUS
IATR/O	DOCTOR/MEDICAL
INFRA	BENEATH
INTER	AMONG
INTRA	INSIDE
ITIS	INFLAMMATION
LACT/O	MILK
LAPAR/O	FLANK/ABDOMEN
LATERO	SIDE
LINGU/O	TONGUE
LYSIS	DISSOLVE
MAL	BAD OR ABNORMAL
MAMM	BREAST
MEGAL/O	LARGE
MY/O	MUSCLES
NAS/O	NOSE
NECR/O	DEATH
NEPHR/O	KIDNEY
NEURO	NERVES/NEUROLOGICAL
OCUL/O	EYE

OMA	TUMOUR
OOPHOR	OVARIES
OPHTHALM	EYE
OPIA	VISION
ORCHI	TESTES
OSIS	CONDITION
OSTE/O	BONE
OT/O	EAR
PAED	CHILD
PERI	AROUND OR DURING
PHAMACO	DRUGS
PHARYNG/O	THROAT
PHLEB/O	VEIN
PHOBIA	FEAR
PLASTY	REPAIR
PLEG/IA	PARALYSIS
PNEUMON	LUNG
POLY	MANY
POST	AFTER
POSTER/I	BEHIND
PSEUD/O	FALSE
PSYCHO	MIND
PULMON	LUNG
RHIN/O	NOSE
SCLER/O	HARD
SCOPE	INSTRUMENT
SUPRA	ABOVE
TACHY	FAST
THERM	HEAT
THORAC	CHEST
THROMB	CLOT OR LUMP
TOMY	INCISION /MAKING A HOLE
URIA	URINE
VEN/O	VEIN
VESICO	BLADDER

Appendix 4

Departments and Personnel

Departments

A & E	Accident & Emergency Department
ANC	Anti Natal Clinic
CCU	Coronary Care Unit
ENT	Ear Nose and Throat
HDU	High Dependency Unit
ICU	Intensive Care Unit
ITU	Intensive Therapy unit
OPD	Out Patient Department
PICU	Paediatric Intensive Care Unit
PN	Post Natal
SCBU	Special Care Baby Unit

Theatres: operating theatres

Recovery: room for patients arriving directly from theatre – still under the effect of anaesthetic.

Medical Teams

Consultant

Usually to obtain membership or fellowship there are a series of examinations in a particular speciality as follows

- MRCP/FRCP
  Member of Royal College of Physicians
  Fellow of Royal College of Physicians

- MRCS/FRCS
  Surgeons

- MRCOG/FRCOG
  Obstetricians and Gynaecologists

- MRC Psych/FRC Psych
  Psychiatrists

Senior Registrars

Until the recent past, most teams included the position of senior registrar. Medical and surgical teams usually have. They have often passed their MRC/FRC exams and are waiting for position as consultants. Records will often show SR for Senior Registrar. The post of Senior Registrar is now changed (see below).

Registrars

Registrars were experienced doctors who are usually working within one speciality. They will be able to undertake more complex procedures and surgery without supervision. Usual abbreviation in records: Reg.

Both Registrar and Senior Registrar are being phased out in favour of Specialist Registrars who complete more intensive and longer training before seeking a consultant post. Usual abbreviation SPR.

Senior house officer

They are less experienced doctors who are usually still doing six month rotation and in the process of choosing particular area of speciality. They will be able to undertake very simple routine procedures and surgery under supervision.

Junior house officer/house officer

They are newly qualified medics who will be completing the traditional six months of medical wards and six months of surgical. There is a change over of staff every six months. Once they have completed this period they can qualify for registration at the General Medical Council.

Nursing teams

Consultants

Some hospitals have consultant nurses. i.e.: senior and experienced nursing personnel

Nurse Managers

Senior nursing staff who will undertake some clinical work in certain hospitals or departments. More generally associated with administration.

Practitioners/Specialists

Experienced nursing personnel who have specialist skills/knowledge which may overlap with those of medical staff. For example: Infection Control Nurses.

Senior Sister (female)/Charge Nurse (Male)

Senior member of team. Usually runs one of more ward depending on speciality and size of department.

Sister/Charge nurse

Often the most senior nurse on a ward or within a department

Staff nurse

Qualified nurse – either RN/RGN Registered nurse or registered general nurse, or EN enrolled nurse. They could be:

- RMN
  registered mental nurse

- RCN
  registered children's nurse

- RM
  registered midwife

- RMHN
  registered mental handicap nurse

  (some of these qualifications are now being phased out)

Student nurses

In training – usually three year course. More experienced have been in training longer. Some complete degrees in nursing and will have less practical experience. Others are more ward based and will have more practical experience but may have less academic knowledge.

Health Care assistants/Nursing auxiliaries

Variety of different names used.Unqualified nursing support staff.
Some are very experienced having been in position for a number of years. Others taught basic skills and restricted in type of work they can do. Some undertake NVQ training.

Some will be able to take pulse temperature and blood pressure readings. All newer members of staff should have been taught to lift properly.

Community nurses

These have similar teams but will include those who have trained as:

HV health visitors
Usually associated with children but can also be involved in care of the elderly. Specialist training in child development.

DN district nurses
Trained in general community care. Wound management, medications review. Being phased out in favour of Community nurses.

School nurses
Specialists who do clinics at schools in rotation.

In addition there are a large number of community based nursing posts to deal with specific medical or nursing problems including:

McMillan/Cancer nurses
Specialist in caring for those with cancer. Often but not always terminal care

Stoma nurses
Will care for those with a colostomy or ileostomy

Diabetic nurses
Care of diabetics. Review and monitoring of insulin

Cardiac care
Usually attached to larger cardiac hospital units

Assist with counselling and advice to cardiac patients

Community Psychiatric Nurses
Specialist mental health nurses who are able to visit users of the psychiatric services at home and provide advice or medication

Nurse Practitioners
Attached to GP surgery providing wide variety of treatments and advice sessions. Particularly wound management and clinics.

Index

Personal Injury and Clinical Negligence:
Some recent titles from
EMIS Professional Publishing

Mentor/Pils

EMIS's major CD resource contains a comprehensive encyclopedia of medicine – from the most basic to fully referenced articles and links to medical websites. Updated regularly by download, Mentor is the ideal reference tool for the lawyer and is written in accessible language.

Ask us for a free demo

Damages

Are you assessing general damages fast enough not to waste precious time?

Quantum of damages is at the heart of all Personal Injury practitioners' work. To assess quantum quickly and accurately is essential not just for the client but for the lawyer seeking to assess risk to put funding in place for the case. This service meets a series of needs not currently met effectively by existing paper or electronic services, digesting the past 10 years' key cases into a simple to use, intelligible format.

Annual service just £99   ISBN 1 85811 264 8

Keep Yourself up to date with EMIS's Newsletters
Ask us for a free sample!

Personal Injury

No 1 Serjeants' Inn

EMIS Professional Publishing is delighted to announce that it provides *the* way to keep up to date with the law and practice of personal injury. In 2002, coverage in the six issues will be comprehensive. The service's new clearer format will ensure that it remains easy to read and use. The editor, Alan Saggerson, is a member of Chambers at No. 1 Serjeants' Inn where he specialises in personal injury litigation with particular emphasis on foreign accidents, conflicts of laws, international travel conventions and the travel industry. He also practices in mainstream personal injury, fatal accident and clinical negligence cases for both claimants and defendants. A free single user licence for Seneca EP is included.

Subscription for one year: £135 includes free single user online access

---

Take both services – and save
– *Damages* and *Personal Injury* combined price £222!

Medico-Legal Journal

Editor: Diana Brahams, Barrister, Old Square Chambers

For the first time, in 1999 EMIS published the *Journal* for the Medico-Legal Society of London, which has provided a forum for lawyers and medics to discuss medico-legal topics for close to a century. The *Journal* provides articles based on lectures given by pre-eminent speakers at the Society. In addition, the *Journal* covers developments in civil procedure as they affect medico-legal work and provide articles on the role of the expert.

£85 includes free single user online access

Health and Safety Law

9 Gough Square Personal Injury and Employment Barristers

Coverage of all that's important in employer's liability

Last year there were over 1 million reported workplace accidents and diseases – for employees and for employers and their insurers this is a vital area of law and practice. The statutory framework consists of specific hazard-based regulations which have been built up steadily since the "six pack" were introduced in 1992. Cases are now regular and substantial – making it vital to keep up to date with regulations and with cases. 9 Gough Square are one of the leading personal injury and employment sets in the country – ideally placed to give a lawyer's eye view of what really matters in health and safety practice.

£80 for newsletter and single user licence for electronic service – £40 with either of the above services

New Books for the Litigator